Judith Clark   Maria Luisa Frisa

DIANA VREELAND AFTER DIANA VREELAND

Marsilio

"NOTHING IS MORE MARVELLOUS THAN SITTING AT A LITTLE
TABLE IN THE GATHERING DUSK IN THE PIAZZA SAN MARCO, THE
GUEST OF THE SIX GOLDEN -BRONZE HORSES PRANCING AWAY
TO PARADISE."

Diana Vreeland

DIANA VREELAND AFTER
DIANA VREELAND

Palazzo Fortuny, Venice
March 10 – June 25, 2012

President
Walter Hartsarich

Board
Vice President
Giorgio Orsoni

Members
Alvise Alverà
Emilio Ambasz
Carlo Fratta Pasini

Director
Gabriella Belli

Executive Secretary
Mattia Agnetti

Palazzo Fortuny
Daniela Ferretti

Exhibition promoted by
Fondazione Musei Civici di Venezia Muve
The Diana Vreeland Estate

In collaboration with

MAURO GRIFONI

VICENZAORO

Technical Partners

think. make. display.

mannequins

Organization and Communication

CIVITA
TRE VENEZIE

With the support of

AGENZIA DEL CONTEMPORANEO

Exhibition curated by
Judith Clark, Maria Luisa Frisa

Commissioned by
Lisa Immordino Vreeland
within the project
Diana Vreeland:
The Eye Has To Travel

Coordination
Daniela Ferretti

Assistants to the Curators
Gabriele Monti
Jenna Rossi-Camus

Exhibition Design
Judith Clark

Organization
Tiziana Alvisi
Elena Santagiustina

Technical support
Francesca Boni

Cabinets
Fusina

Mannequins
La Rosa Mannequins

Wigs
Angelo Seminara For Davines
Ana Fernández
Akira Yamada

Resarch in collaboration with
"Il progetto nella moda/
Italian Studies in Fahion Design",
research unit of the Università di Venezia,
Scientific Director Mario Lupano

Press Office
Fondazione Musei Civici di Venezia
Riccardo Bon
with
AE Media Comunicazione
DELOS, Servizi per la cultura

Civita Tre Venezie
Valeria Regazzoni

Promotion
Silvia Negretti
Alessandro Paolinelli

Administration
Antonella Ballarin
with
Piero Calore
Carla Povelato
Francesca Rodella

Lenders
Associazione Dolomiten Freunde -
Amici delle Dolomiti
Class Editori
Collection of Michael H. Berkowitz
Collezione Museo di Storia Naturale,
Venice
© Fondation Pierre Bergé -
Yves Saint Laurent, Paris
Fondazione Archivio Emilio Pucci
Fondazione Ottavio e Rosita Missoni
Fundación Cristóbal Balenciaga Fundazioa
Museo di Palazzo Mocenigo -
Centro Studi di Storia del Tessuto
e del Costume, Venice
The Costume Institute of
The Metropolitan Museum of Art,
New York
The Diana Vreeland Estate
Valentino S.p.A.

Collezione Cecilia Matteucci Lavarini
Andrea de Marchi
Estate of Simone Valsecchi ARCHI-V-E
Cesare Fabbri
Maria Luisa Frisa
Judith Clark Costume Gallery Archive
Martin Kamer, Switzerland
Katell le Bourhis Collection
Gabriele Monti
Luigino Rossi
Frederick Vreeland

Thanks to
Ministero per i Beni e la Attività Culturali
Servizio III - Direzione Generale per
il Paesaggio, le Belle Arti, l'Architettura
e l'Arte Contemporanee/Servizio V-
Direzione Generale per la qualità
e la tutela del Paesaggio, l'Architettura
e l'Arte Contemporanee
Soprintendenza Speciale per il Patrimonio
Storico, Artistico ed Etnoantropologico
e per il Polo Museale della città di Venezia
e dei Comuni della Gronda lagunare

Special thanks to
Pierre Bergé, President, and
Philippe Mugnier, General Director,
Fondation Pierre Bergé - Yves Saint
Laurent
Javier González de Durana,
General Director, Museo Cristóbal
Balenciaga, Getaria
Harold Koda, Curator-in-Charge, The
Costume Institute of The Metropolitan
Museum of Art, New York
Alexander Vreeland, President,
The Diana Vreeland Estate

The Fortuny Museum is opening its exhibition season with an extraordinary show devoted to the figure of Diana Vreeland, fashion editor and editor-in-chief, from 1936 until the beginning of the 1970s, of important magazines like *Harper's Bazaar* and *Vogue*, and then, up until her death in 1989, special consultant to the Costume Institute of the Metropolitan Museum of Art in New York.

A woman who revolutionized the fashion culture of half a century. A figure both loved and contested in the fashion community, but one who has left a deep mark on it. As the great photographer Richard Avedon said at the time of her death: "she was and remains the only genius fashion editor."

The exhibition devoted to her and curated by Judith Clark and Maria Luisa Frisa investigates many aspects of her work and offers new keys to the interpretation of her style and her thought. It does not limit itself to presenting clothes, although there are many beautiful garments there to be admired, but brings the objects and their "aura" into prominence, showing that fashion is a complex phenomenon and a favored vantage point for the interpretation of tastes and trends.

On display in the exhibition are clothes that are part of the history of fashion and that have been brought to Italy for the first time, coming from the Metropolitan Museum of Art in New York, the Fondation Pierre Bergé-Yves Saint Laurent and the Museo Cristóbal Balenciaga as well as from collections of private individuals and fashion designers. Thus the route through the exhibition takes the form of a genuine three-dimensional reflection on Diana Vreeland's museological contribution to exhibiting and curating fashion, through a design that identifies and utilizes the elements of curatorial grammar developed by Vreeland.

Thanks go to all those who have made this exhibition possible.

Walter Hartsarich

It is hard for us to imagine a better setting than Palazzo Fortuny to present the first retrospective devoted to Diana Vreeland, an extraordinary personality who in the century that has just come to an end brought about a radical change in the world of fashion magazines and exhibitions.

A powerful visual imagination, a taste for experimentation, an obsessive attention to detail and a boundless curiosity are just some of the affinities that can be found between Mariano Fortuny and his exuberant "guest."

A restless spirit, fascinated by the Belle Époque, the Ballets Russes, orientalism and the creative frenzy of the 1960s, Diana Vreeland drew her lifeblood from a continuous mixing of styles, periods and disciplines that differed greatly from one another.

Diana Vreeland's complex, visionary alphabet has been analyzed with academic rigor and carefully reassembled in the layout of the exhibition by Judith Clark and Maria Luisa Frisa.

Thanks to their enthusiasm, the exhibition *Diana Vreeland After Diana Vreeland* is able to fully convey the fascination, the ideas and the vision of an outstanding figure.

With regard to the organization of the event in Venice, many difficulties would not have been overcome without the capacities for coordination of Tiziana Alvisi and Elena Santagiustina, the steadfastness of Silvia Carrer and the constant technical support of Francesca Boni.

Special thanks must go to Harold Koda of the Costume Institute of the Metropolitan Museum of Art in New York, to Pierre Bergé and Philippe Mugnier of the Fondation Pierre Bergé-Yves Saint Laurent in Paris and to Javier González de Durana of the Museo Cristóbal Balenciaga in Getaria, without whose contribution this exhibition would not have been possible.

Daniela Ferretti
Lisa Immordino Vreeland

Volume published on the occasion
of the exhibition
DIANA VREELAND AFTER DIANA VREELAND

Book Concept
Maria Luisa Frisa

Iconographic Research
Valentina Meneghello

Graphic Design
Alessandro Gori.Laboratorium

Iconographic Coordination
Serena Becagli.Laboratorium
with
Alexis Myers

Cover
Unfolding Vreeland artwork
Alessandro Gori.Laboratorium MMXII
featuring Vreeland's portraits
by George Hoyningen-Huene,
© Ricky Horst, late 1930s-early 1940s
and Priscilla Rattazzi, 1982,
courtesy Priscilla Rattazzi

Photographs on the flaps, inside cover
and inside back cover, pages 1, 240
Francesco De Luca
Styling
Francesco Casarotto
Mannequins
La Rosa Mannequins

Ottoman robe in blue velvet with gold
embroidery, late 19th century; Evening
cape in red silk taffeta, Biki, late
1960s-early 1970s (owned by Maria
Callas); Semi-formal woman's robe in
aquamarine satin embroidered with
butterflies and flowers, China, first half
of 19th century; Black velvet redingote
with black taffeta lining, Balenciaga, haute
couture, no. 33191, circa 1948. Cecilia
Matteucci Lavarini Collection

Missoni knitted dress, spring-summer
collection 1969; Missoni knitted
ensamble, spring-summer collection
1971. Fondazione Ottavio e Rosita
Missoni

Silk chiffon dress printed with "Quadrati"
pattern, Emilio Pucci, 1968. Fondazione
Archivio Emilio Pucci

Yellow plastic disks and fringes minidress,
Paco Rabanne, second half of 1960s;
Embroidered silk coat, Chanel, label
"Cannes-31 Rue Cambon-Paris-Biarritz,"
no. 5046, 1920s (owned by Eleonora
Duse). Estate of Simone Valsecchi
ARCHI-V-E

Translations
Huw Evans

Editing
in.pagina s.r.l. - Mestre-Venice

© 2012 by Marsilio Editori® s.p.a.
in Venice

ISBN 88-317-1279

www.marsilioeditori.it

Photolitography
Fotolita Veneta, San Martino Buonalbergo
(VR)

Printed by
Studio Fasoli, Verona
for Marsilio Editori® s.p.a., Venice

Contents

MARIA LUISA FRISA
After Pictures 1[1]

These photographs selected run the gamut of many styles: studio portraits, paparazzi and news pictures, advertisements, and photos, though posed, done in natural light. Many have been published before—in some cases the originals were unobtainable or have been lost forever—many have been reproduced from newspaper and magazine pages. This is a potpourri which I chose to amuse and perhaps please the reader.
(Diana Vreeland)

We know that a picture is but a space in which a variety of images, none of them original, blend and clash.
(Sherrie Levine)

The title of this book and of the associated exhibition, *Diana Vreeland After Diana Vreeland*, came to mind while visiting *Mayhem*, the exhibition by Sherrie Levine that opened last November at the Whitney Museum in New York. It included one of the artist's seminal works, *After Walker Evans*, from 1981.

"After," in the work of Sherrie Levine, signifies the transformation and recontextualization of images and objects in order to create something new. In the exhibition, put together by the artist as a coherent project aimed at defining a galaxy of old and new works, that word triggered a montage which was the starting point for an extraordinary sequence of associations and reflections. Associations and reflections not just within the poetics of the artist, considered one of the principal exponents of appropriation art, or on an artistic gesture that has its fundamental precedents in the readymades of Marcel Duchamp or the actions of the Situationist International, but also with respect to the various aspects of an attitude shared by many members of the more recent generations of artists, i.e. all those practices of editing and montage that have found a precise definition in the theories of postproduction put forward by Nicolas Bourriaud.

Diana Vreeland is such a charismatic and unique figure in the history of fashion that her personality runs the risk of remaining petrified in the account of the incredible life she led between Paris, London and New York. Frozen, again, that extraordinary story, in the continual re-proposition of her memorable words and actions. In an often stereotyped narrative that in the end does not concern itself over much with investigating the real importance of Diana Vreeland's work, first as fashion editor of *Harper's Bazaar* and editor of *Vogue America*, then as fashion consultant to the Metropolitan in New York.

"The archeology of things to come" is a wonderfully evocative oxymoron that Daniel Birnbaum uses to speak of the work of the curator and, more in particular, that of Hans Ulrich Obrist in his afterword to the collection of interviews conducted by Obrist himself in 2008 and significantly entitled *A Brief History of Curating*.[2] The writings of the critic and the action of the curator are acts that plan and recount in the present, following a personal itinerary, affected by the suggestions with which existing materials resound. It is the ideas, the words, the objects, the images that are recomposed in the dimension of the presentation of a statement. To produce an innovative vision the curator acts on settled elements that belong to the past, that have been temporarily forgotten, put aside, but are waiting to be reactivated, brought back into circulation through a gaze that is capable of consigning them once again to the future, given new names in their new location. Critics and curators have the ability to tell a story, but in recounting their project and the suggestions generated by their materials express themselves through that "understanding by doing" that is, today, a fundamental part of any creative process.

Understanding by doing has revealed itself to be a way of approaching Diana Vreeland. Someone who started out from the extraordinary gallery of her imagination. The Vreeland method was triggered by a vision that had to take on form and image. She was not interested in what others thought, whether they were her photographers or the curators of the Metropolitan. It was her vision that was central.[3] She herself recounted how she liked to mix up the images and bodies of models in search of the "perfect whole," of an ensemble constructed to convey an idea of style visually. Through images, novel montages, the attempt to design landscapes of double-page spreads that would communicate impressions and emotions. It was she who gave the 1960s an image.

The first to turn models into personalities. And it was Benedetta Barzini, one of her many discoveries, along with Twiggy, Penelope Tree, Veruschka and Marisa Berenson, who interpreted, in the *Vogue* of August 1964, the spirit of young, fashionable girls. Then, in *Vogue* again, appeared the Chicerinos (a neologism of her own invention that combined the term chic with a diminutive form), who included Françoise Hardy, Catherine Spaak and Barbra Streisand. For it was she, in fact, who launched the fashion for using actresses as models. She was curious about everything, she looked at everything without prejudice. She was interested in Italy, in its fashion, its handicrafts and its "beautiful people." Irene Brin was the Rome editor of *Harper's Bazaar*.[4]

The visual essay, made up of a series of images chosen from the vast Vreeland repertoire—not just the magazines, *Bazaar* and *Vogue*, but also the catalogs of her exhibitions, which reproduced the gleaming phantasmagoria of her inventions in 2D, and then the books, like *Allure*, designed to put in order her obsessions, the figures that crowded her imagination—is constructed on fifteen guidewords. Many of these words allude to her passions, while others are her inventions, and yet others have become, thanks to the use she

made of them, indispensable elements in the definition of fashion and its language today. To the point of being worn out and emptied of meaning, of becoming an affected diction of fashion. There are words that reflect the conscious process of construction of Vreeland's mythology, like "RED," "SELF-STYLING," "OBSESSIONS," "SPOTS"; there are words that do not just punctuate the features in magazines, but also identify the elements (and the attitudes) that have peppered Vreeland's declarations about her presentations: "BIZARRE," "EXOTIC," "COLORQUAKE," "FLAMBOYANT," "PERFECTION," "ALLURE," "PERSONALITIES," "PIZZAZZ," "CHIC," "PARISIAN"; out of all these there is one word that sums up the attitude with which Vreeland always approached and used fashion: "INTERPRETATION." The images follow the words freely, and fragments of texts follow the images in a porous montage. The words, which are revealed from the outset for what they are, a pretext, are organized into a map that also takes in all the extraordinary personalities with whom Diana Vreeland held a dialog over the course of her life. In a galaxy that covers not only the fashion but the whole culture of much of the last century.

Looking back over all the materials that bear Diana Vreeland's mark, we realize that they are an account of the continuous present of fashion. They are a series of obsessions, desires and dreams that have taken shape from an idea of style and fashion, but also an account in sequence of all the moments of the life she lived. A trailblazing one, that no longer seems possible today. Sliding constantly between the roles of fashion editor and fashion curator, Vreeland was able to play the card of interpretation, to the point of creating within the museum that overlap of presentation between place of cultural reflection and place of shopping which was to become fully established in the second half of the 1990s and to last right through the first decade of the 21st century, in the era of "total living."

Debora Silverman's book *Selling Culture*, is a very harsh attack on Vreeland's work at the Met, which places the exhibitions she staged within the perspective of "the new aristocracy of taste in Reagan's America." In the introduction, on the subject of the retrospective devoted to Yves Saint Laurent, she declares: "Visitors to the Saint Laurent show found the museum exhibition curiously indistinguishable from the same designer's display at fashionable department stores such as Bloomingdale's and Neiman-Marcus. The galleries at the Met were not organized according to a chronological

development, befitting an artist's 'retrospective.' [...] Instead, the galleries were arranged by color schemes, and by the 'timeless' divisions that structure a certain type of woman's day [...]. Vreeland's Saint Laurent show succeeded, not as museum education, but as a giant advertising campaign for French haute couture [...]."[5] A year later, for *Art in America*,[6] Robert Storr reviewed Silverman's book and launched his own attack on Vreeland's work at the Met, clear even from the title of his article, "Unmaking History at the Costume Institute." "Pitching to the largest possible public, she still follows at the Metropolitan the merchandising motto that once guided her at 'Vogue': GIVE 'EM WHAT THEY NEVER KNEW THEY WANTED," wrote Storr, who fiercely criticized the opulence and visionary excess of Vreeland's displays because they seemed to give greater emphasis to atmosphere than to informative content.[7]

And yet in Vreeland's "aggressive frivolity" there is the mark of someone who had also been able to find the force of the curatorial act, who did not pretend to relate "history," but instead set out to interweave elements of the past in unprecedented ways in order to spark off reflections on the present. In 1976, on the occasion of Vreeland's fourth exhibition at the Metropolitan, *American*

Women of Style, New York Magazine[8] devoted a review to the event that was also a reflection on the new role of the museum and exhibitions with respect to fashion: "The museum's new fashion power doesn't end with its control of immortality. Its costume shows are involved with resurrection as well. Edging out the fashion magazines, the Paris runway, and the discotheque, it has become the launching pad for new style trends inspired by exhibits of bygone body wear." It mattered little if among the portraits, memorabilia and clothes of the ten icons of style in the exhibition there were also copies, or if omissions had been made in the selection of the objects. What did matter, what was at the heart of the project, what in the last analysis was on display, was the critical view and act of interpretation that still define today the highly personal curatorial grammar of Vreeland, always excessive and dramatic.

"Performance is all I cared about as a child and it's all I care about now. I don't go to see a play to see a great play, I go to see a great interpretation," she declared in *Allure*.[9] Vreeland appropriated images through violent operations of cropping and then recomposed them in sequences capable of tracing new trajectories and telling stories that very often had nothing in common with the visual and narrative universes from which they were drawn. It is no coincidence that Diana Vreeland associated some of her memorable exhibitions with complex publishing projects, realized after the closure of the exhibitions. Not catalogs therefore, but genuine visual essays in 2D that reutilized not just the images of the displays, but also elements of the exhibitions themselves: I am thinking for example of the photographic essay by Irving Penn, published in 1977[10] and based on the exhibition *The 10s, The 20s, The 30s: Inventive Clothes 1909-1939*. In this book the gallery of pictures is simultaneously a celebration of the Parisian couture of the early decades of the 20th century and an exploration of the mannequin, the body of fashion and a powerful device capable of interpreting the atmosphere and the design of a garment.

Vreeland's approach to publishing affirmed the power of the double-page spread, which thus also seemed to become the preferred means of fixing the exhibition— temporary event *par excellence*, impossible to place in the archives—and its grammar (the photos by Duane Michals in the catalog of the retrospective devoted to Yves Saint Laurent[11] are not of the exhibition itself, but propose another version, with drapes that hide the set, wrap the mannequins and allude to the genesis in muslin of the clothes that they display). Thus the fashion exhibition acts not just by crystallizing and monumentalizing the past, but also by nurturing and defining new trends, for it is a device that restrains and simultaneously amplifies the vision and the voice of the curator. As the title of the article that appeared in *New York Magazine* on January 12 1976 suggests, it is a question of *exhibition-ism*.

Notes

1   *Pictures* is the title of the legendary exhibition organized by Douglas Crimp in 1977 at the Artists Space in New York. On display was the work of five artists, Tony Brauntuch, Jack Goldstein, Sherrie Levine, Robert Longo and Philip Smith, who had made an impression on Crimp through their common interest "in the photographically-based mass media as a source to be raided and re-used. *Pictures* was the forerunner of an appropriationist current that became strongly associated with certain commercial galleries in New York. Metro Pictures, for instance, which represented key figures such as Richard Prince and Cindy Sherman [...]" (David Evans [ed.], *Appropriation*. London-Cambridge MA: Whitechapel - The MIT Press, pp. 12-3).

2   Daniel Birnbaum, "The Archeology of Things to Come," in Hans Ulrich Obrist, *A Brief History of Curating*. Zurich-Dijon: JRPRingier-Les Presses du réel, 2008, pp. 234-9.

3   In September 1988 *Vogue Italy* published an article on Diana Vreeland, in an issue on high fashion in Rome and Paris. In it Gini Alhadeff describes her as brilliant and unique. And it is her friends who talk about her: among them Horst, Hubert de Givenchy, Pierre Bergé and Valentino. The article begins: "While students were fighting with the police in Berkeley, Diana Vreeland sent Richard Avedon to the mountains in the north of Japan to photograph a white cashmere cloak for *Vogue*." DV style.

4   Irene Brin was intercepted in New York, on Park Avenue, one afternoon in 1950, thanks to what she was wearing: a skirt and jacket by Fabiani with a hat by Fath. Diana Vreeland stopped her in the street, demanding with passion: "Where did you get it, who made it?"

5   Debora Silverman, *Selling Culture: Bloomingdale's, Diana Vreeland, and the New Aristocracy of Taste in Reagan's America*. New York: Pantheon books, 1986, pp. 3-5.

6   Robert Storr, "Unmaking History at the Costume Institute," *Art in America*, February 1987, pp. 15-23.

7   I am reminded of the *24-Hour Museum*, a project by Francesco Vezzoli and AMO for Prada. The reflection of one of the most interesting of today's artists on the relationship between the eternity of the museum and the transitoriness of fashion; between the brevity of a provocative gesture and its efficacy in the duration permitted by the net. The absoluteness of the museum which, if it wants to go on existing, has to deal with a point of view that cannot always be the same.

8   Joan Kron, "Exhibition-ism: History as Fashion Power," *New York Magazine*, January 12, 1976, pp. 76-8.

9   Diana Vreeland, with Christopher Hemphill, *Allure*. New York: Doubleday, 1980, p. 104.

10   Irving Penn, *Inventive Paris Clothes 1909-1939*, with text by Diana Vreeland. New York: The Viking Press, 1977.

11   *Yves Saint Laurent*, catalog of the exhibition curated by Diana Vreeland (New York, The Costume Institute at The Metropolitan Museum of Art, December 6, 1983-September 2, 1984). New York: The Metropolitan Museum of Art - C.N. Potter, 1983.

After Pictures 2

Red is the great clarifier—bright, cleansing, and revealing.

It makes a other colors beautiful. I can't imagine becoming bored with red—It would be like becoming bored with the person you love.

All my life I've pursued the perfect red. I can never get painters to mix it for me. It's exactly as if I'd said, "I want rococo with a spot of Gothic in it and a bit of Buddhist temple"—they have *no* idea what I'm talking about. About the best red is to copy the color of a child's cap in any Renaissance portrait.

I loathe red with *any* orange in it—although, curiously enough, I also loathe orange *without* red in it. When I say "orange," I don't mean yellow-orange, I mean *red*-orange—the orange of Bakst and Diaghilev, the orange that changed the *century*.

When I arrived in America, I had these very dark red nails which some people objected to, but then some people object to absolutely everything. The point is that they were absolutely clear and perfect. There was only one other woman in New York with perfect nails, and that was Mona Williams, who had a manicurist come to her every evening.

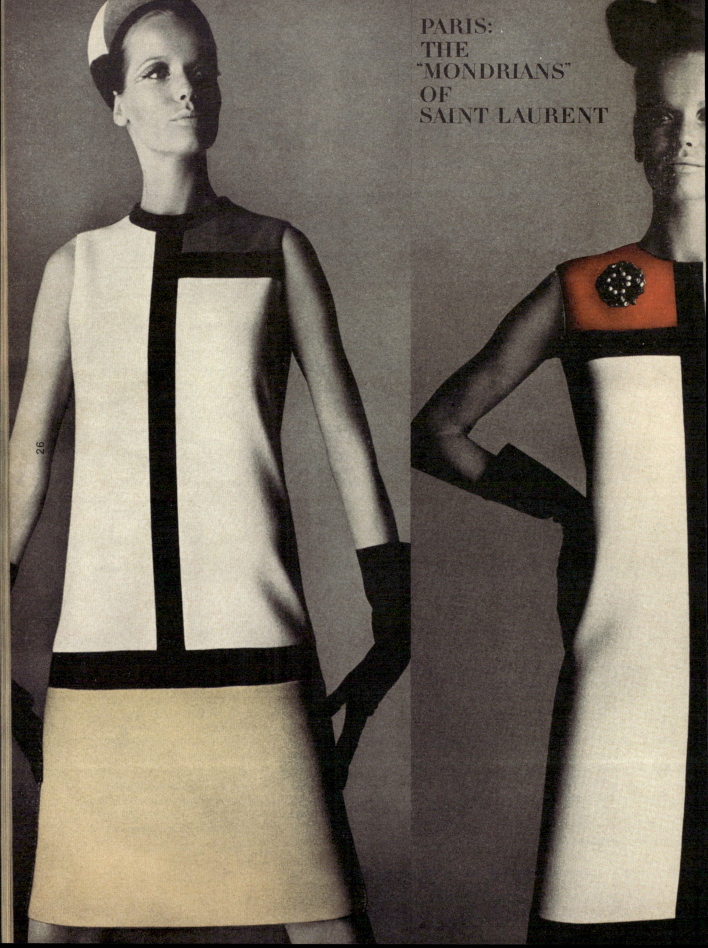

PARIS:
THE
"MONDRIANS"
OF
SAINT LAURENT

Clean, terse, white jersey rectangles.
Mondrian proportions—bold black
tapes, blocks of colour laid on
like fresh paint.... Bottle the spirit of this
collection, label it Y—as in Yves, as in
yummy-new-perfume—and Yes, as soft, as
charming, as all-out alluring as you'd
expect. Wafting this way soon.
Far left: Elongated proportions—
black Mondrian tapes and white jersey
extended past the hipbone...
beige to the hem...one shoulder squared
in charcoal. At Neiman-Marcus; I. Magnin.
Saint Laurent diamonds-of-colour casquette.
Left: Heightened proportions—
T of black tapes barred
above the bosom...black-ruled hem...
Saint Laurent brilliants on the bright red
shoulder. Bonwit Teller; Neiman-Marcus;
I. Magnin; Holt Renfrew of Canada.
Right: Proportions blocked out in colour—
blue on the shoulder...
red through the torso...white skirt...band
of yellow hem...Mondrian tapes ruling all.
At Joseph Horne; I. Magnin. Both pages,
Racine wool jersey dresses.

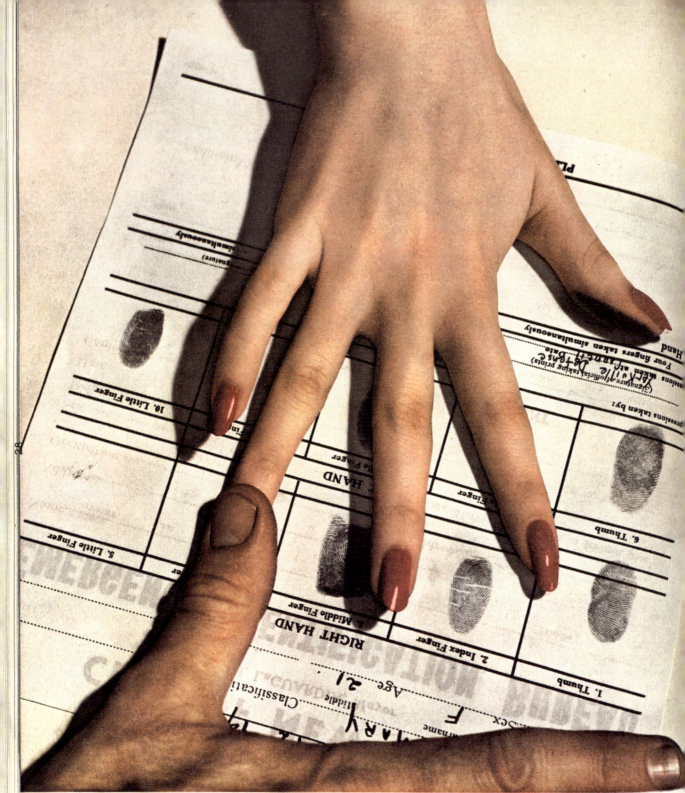

KODACHROME BY HOYNINGEN-HUENE

FINGERPRINTS

The Office of Civilian Defense has asked all Americans to be fingerprinted. It is not compulsory, but patriotic citizens are flocking into O.C.D. offices all over the country to stamp their fingers on the records for identification purposes. Our camera focused on one lovely hand in the act. The lady's nails are brightly lacquered with Chen Yu's Dragon's Blood polish. Bonwit Teller.

Make it big!

What we remember most about Hollywood is the glamour and the romance they gave us. How they glorified their heroes and worshiped their heroines. Those beautiful women, those handsome men. For Hollywood, everything was larger than life, bigger than anything before or since.

The diamonds were bigger, the fur were thicker; the silks, velvets, satins, chiffons were richer and silkier. There were miles of ostrich feathers, maribou, white fox, and sable; miles of bugle beads, diamante, and sequins. Hollywood was paved with glitter, shine, and glory. Everything was an exaggeration of history, fiction, and the whole wide extraordinary world. After all, nothing was too good for Hollywood, and for Hollywood nothing was too good for the people.

Of course, much was the influence of Diaghilev. The flavor, the extravagance, the *allure*, the excitement, the passion, the smash, the clash, the *crash*... this man smashed the atom! His influence on Paris was complete. [...] The colors! Before then, red had never been red and violet had never been violet. They were always slightly... grayed. But these women's clothes in the Bois were of colors as sharp as a knife: red red, *violent* violet, orange [...]. And the *fabrics* —the silks, the satins, and the brocades, embroidered with seed pearls and braid, shot with silver and gold and trimmed with fur and lace—were of an Oriental *splendeur*. There's never been such luxury since. These women *looked* rich.

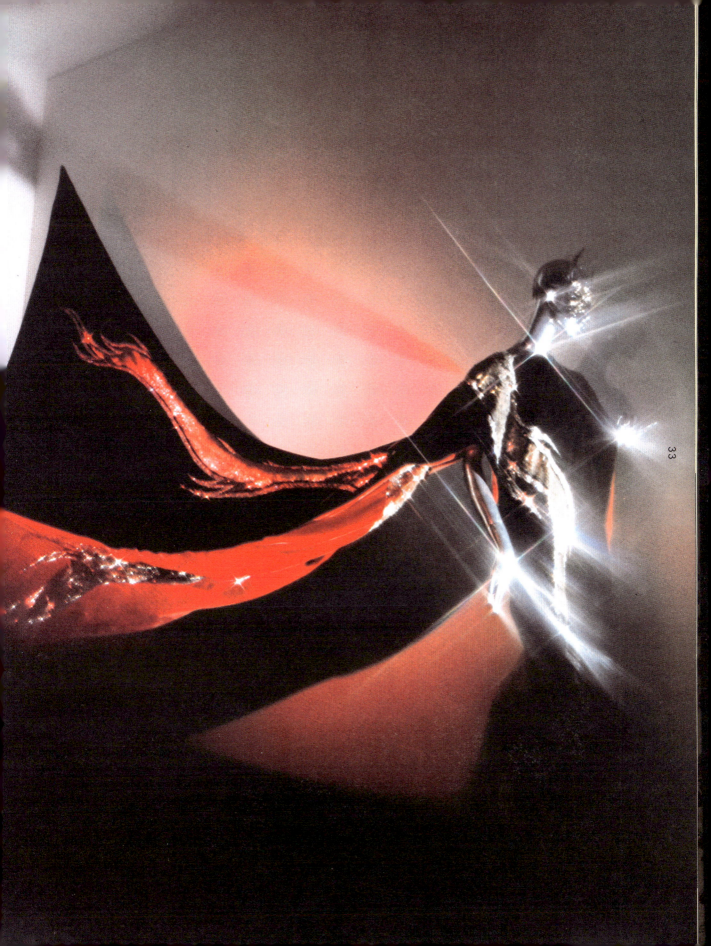

33

September 16, 1968
Re: SERPENTS
Don't forget the serpent...
The serpent should be on every finger
and all wrists and all everywhere...
The serpent is the motif of the hours in
jewellery...
We cannot see enough of them...

December 3, 1969
subject: WILD LIFE
At last after all this time of talking and asking, we have received
a list of animals that appertain to our business that are in danger
of extinction:
<u>All Spotted Cats</u>
Cheetah
Leopard
Jaguar
Ocelot

I looked down—and it was a *cheetah*. And beside the cheetah was Josephine *Baker*! [...] She was alone with the cheetah on a lead. She was so beautifully dressed. [...] The cheetah, naturally, took the lead, and Josephine, with those *long* black legs, was *dragged* down three flights of stairs as fast as she could go, and that's *fast*. [...] The driver opened the door; she let go of the lead; the cheetah *whooped*, took *one* leap into the back of the Rolls, with Josephine right behind; the door closed... and they were off! Ah! What a gesture! I've never seen anything like it. It was speed at its best, and style! Style was a great thing in those days.

Nicholas Vreeland captured this portrait of his grandmother and her maid, Yvonne Duval Brown, in the dining room.

Harper's BAZAAR

American Summer Fashions

The Paris Scene

May 1948

VOGUE

SEPT. 15

5¢

THE ORNAMENTAL EYE

THE PARIS FASCINATION

VOGUE'S SECOND REPORT
ON THE NEW
FRENCH CLOTHES

IN THE U.S.A.
LOOKS IN THE LEAD FOR
THE NIFTY
AMERICAN

THE ELIGIBLE BACHELORS OF BRITAIN
AND BY CLEVELAND AMORY—"MRS. PAYSON'S BALL PARK"

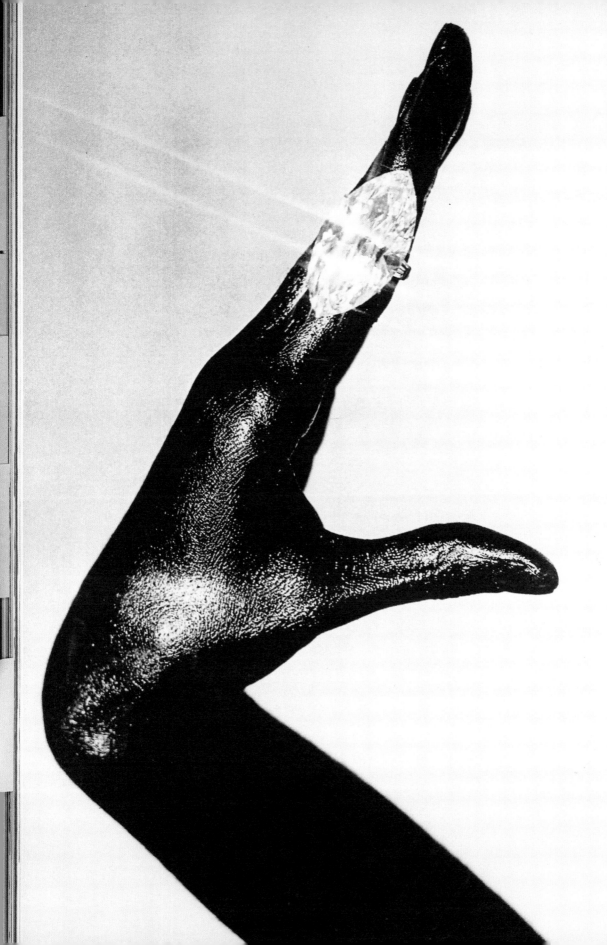

I have astigmatism, like El Greco. I'm not comparing myself with El Greco for a minute, except that we both have the same physical disability. Partly because of his disability he saw things that most people don't see. I see all sorts of things that you don't see.

Violet is a color I really like, But then I like almost every color. I have an eye for color—perhaps the most exceptional gift I have.

Subject: SHADES OF PURPLE
I do think that we should specialize in magenta, bright red, violet, purple, etc.
We all feel it.
We all know it.
But it never seems to come in the book.
We made a special effort for January 1 and it looked very well if you want to look back and see—why don't I see it coming in anymore.

Clean, clear, and Oriental colors... Lots of blue in every collection: Bristol, enamel, and the grey-blues... The Cardin greens—pale avocado to jade to Erin Go Bragh, and all tonal stops between... Gold metallics rampant... Throbs of violet... Pink magenta with plenty of pink and magenta... Original and amusing tweeds and suit fabrics: triangle checks on grey-to-charcoal tweed... a sleek little blouse of guinea-hen feathers with a steel-grey tweed suit... Black ostrich for a taupe evening suit...

Luscious petticoats

There's a fashion among fashion writers
to use appetizing adjectives.
Were you — gentle readers — to take us literally,
you'd see yourselves looking
good enough to eat.

is Delicious

A delectable crinoline

HENRY ROX

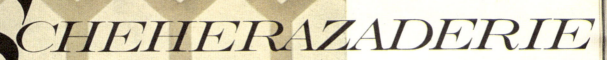

SCHEHERAZADERIE

The fascination never stops . . . and it's new again in this year's fashion . . . the lure of Eastern seraglios and Arab nights; of the Sweet Waters of Asia—the Sea of Marmara, the Bosporus, and the Golden Horn; of Delacroix's North Africa with its splendid diaphanous skies, a light that's pink and orange and silvery. . . . The exuberant colours of Bakst and Poiret—orange and restless amaranth, potent pinks and yellows, porcelain blues and greens. Colour on colour, texture on texture, pattern on pattern. . . . The powerful implication of languor; gauzy chemises, fluent robes, and *chalwar* trousers worn against the most delicate skins . . . bodies slender but rounded with high, arched bosoms . . . small finely moulded feet laden with jewels. . . . The odalisque attitudes of Matisse. . . . Kohl around the eyes, the undiluted scents of rose, patchouli, ambergris, and musk. . . . It's all here, deliciously translated in the modern idiom of at-home clothes, clothes for *la vie privée*, immediate, contemporary, with all the indolent grace of Turquerie to charm the sheik at home.

FAROUCHE PRINTS.... GREAT RINGS.... A CASCADE OF ROSES.... KHALKHAL ANKLE BRACELETS TO DISCOURAGE RUNNING AWAY

Away from the Sultan's harem . . . or at any rate that was the original idea; the present point is to stay at home as reigning favourite in billowy *chalwar* trousers—vivid yellow, fuchsia, and green—with a slashed blouse of pink, blue, and olive on white, worn over a shirt of white cotton eyelet. By Salvador Morrel; of Gourdon silk. At Bonwit Teller; organdie cap by Adolfo. Ropes of pearls by Marvella. Bracelets by Fabiola. Ankle bracelets by Robert Originals. Belt by Ben-King. Rings by Richelieu; Joseph Warner; Cadoro; Fabiola. Fingernails on these pages gilded with Dorothy Gray Rogue's Gold nail enamel.

Mel Ferrer as Luis Bello, the bullfighter, broken by defeat

Harper's BAZAAR

Summer Brides...
Summer
on the land

73

June 1944

50 CENTS
60 CENTS IN CANADA
2/6 IN LONDON

THE CONDÉ NAST PUBLICATIONS *Inc.*

To	BARON DE GUNZBURG	From	MRS. VREELAND
	MRS. SIMPSON		
Copy to	MRS. SCHIFF	Subject:	KNITS

To BARON DE GUNZBURG
MRS. SIMPSON
Copy to MRS. SCHIFF
MRS. MELLEN
MRS. DI MONTEZEMOLO
MRS. HOVEY
MISS DONOVAN
MRS. INGERSOLL
MISS MC KENNA
MRS. BUTLER
MISS WINKELHORN
MISS HAYS
MR. DUHE
MRS. BLACKMON
MISS CANNE
MISS MIRABELLA
MRS. FRANKEL
MRS. BOOTE
MRS. LOEW GROSS

MISS SLAVIN
MISS MACRAE

From MRS. VREELAND

Date June 10,1970

Subject: KNITS

Of course Italy is a marvelous place for knitted clothes.

The thing that catches the eye the most is the various patterns of knits -- by this I don't mean colourings, I mean the different textures whether they are a form of silk, wool or a mixture -- none of them looked the same and all of them have enormous personality.

I do think that our knits are fairly monotonous, although very good, but they all look alike.

I am speaking of the actual knitting.

THE CONDÉ NAST PUBLICATIONS Inc.

To   BARON DE GUNZBURG   From   MRS. VREELAND   Date

          MRS. SIMPSON   April 14, 1969

Copy to MRS. SCHIFF   Subject:

          MRS. MELLEN

          MRS. DI MONTEZEMOLO

          MRS. HOVEY

          MISS DONOVAN

          MRS. INGERSOLL

          MISS MC KENNA

          MRS. BUTLER

          MISS WINKELHORN

          MISS HAYS

          MR. DUHÉ

          MRS. BLACKMON

          MISS CANNÉ

          MISS MIRABELLA

          MRS. FRANKEL

Let's promote grey.

For everything.

At the present moment how much grey have we got?

BROADCLOTH APPEARS FOR EVENING IN BRICK-DUST AND PALE CHAMPAGNE— AND NOTE HOW STRAIGHT AND SLIM THE SILHOUETTE—HOW CA... ...ECT THIS WOULD BE FOR A LITTLE DINNER AND THE THEATRE

HATTIE CARNEGIE. MARTHA WEATHERED, CHICAGO. COIFFURE, GUILLAUME, ELIZABETH ARDEN

RUG BY MYBOR

MAN RAY

VIONNET

FACONNÉ VELVET, CUT TO LAY BARE A WOMAN'S SHOULDERS

THE MOLDED DRESSES THERE ARE FULL SKIRTS SPREADING REGALLY LIKE THIS ONE OF

SALON DE COUTURE, BONWIT TELLER. I. MAGNIN, CALIFORNIA

Harper's BAZAAR

Incorporating Junior Bazaar

The Gala Season
Christmas Gifts
Lingerie

82

November 1949
60 Cents

VOGUE

B. 1

AMERICANA ISSUE

VOGUE'S PICK OF THE GREAT AMERICAN CLOTHES

a coast-to-coast fashion report

Bargains in chic U.S.A.

*P*anache of ostrich . . . rows of pearls. *right:* a proper dream of Ascot. *Below:* Black velvet and white organza ribboned with black satin. In hand: a parasol. *Below right:* White lace dress with a blue taffeta sash. On top, a saucer of blue and white taffeta roses.

Above, far right: More hats. Ermine tails gilding a lily-white crêpe and satin dress. This time the hat is a swoop of black velvet, discreetly flirty.

130

CECIL BEA

THE PLASTIC GIANTESSES OF THE PARIS EXPOSITION
WITH ALIX'S BAROQUE VELVET — SUPPLELY DRAPED

LUCHA TRUEL

AND LELONG'S ORIENTAL COLORS IN CREPE AND
RIBBONS, VEILED — PLASTERED ON LIKE PAPER

"ALLURE" is a word very
few people use nowadays, but it's
something that exists. Allure holds
you, doesn't it? Whether it's a gaze or
a glance in the street or a face in the
crowd or someone sitting opposite
you at lunch... you are held. [...] Now
I think it's something around you,
like a perfume or like a scent. It's like
memory... it pervades.

I adore artifice, but I also adore perfection.
And, as you know, the most perfect body in the world will take
on something you don't want when it assumes a certain position.
Therefore, it's got to be retouched. For the same reason,
I *approve* of plastic surgery.
None of my friends can understand why I haven't had it done
myself. I have my own reasons. But the only point is, now it's
normal as taking an aspirin. Whereas, only fifteen years ago...

At *Harper's Bazaar*, we often used
composite pictures. We'd done it for years. I got
the idea from fashion illustration. In Paris,
long before I went into business, I used to pose
for so many artists you can't imagine—always
from the head down. It was known as "figure
modeling". They never used my face, but I know
how to wear clothes and I've always *adored* to
pose.

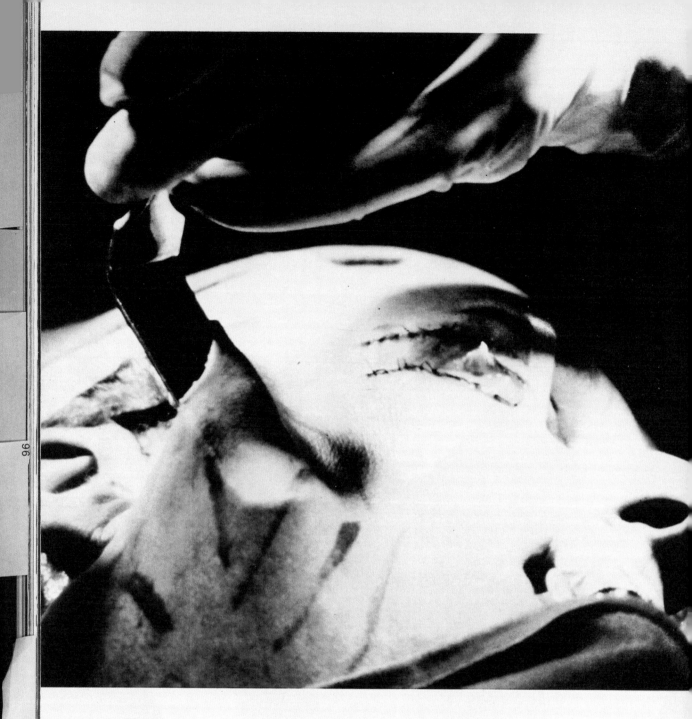

They couldn't publish half the things I did on *Vogue*. I remember Elliott Erwitt did some pictures for us of an eye-lift operation. *That* was a scene. The pictures were shown to various members of the staff. One left immediately to throw up, others were gagging and carrying on, others . . . these were *professional* women working on a *woman's* magazine, you understand—not a gaggle of housewives. It was *un*-believable!

Now most of what looked like blood was Mercurochrome, because it's a special operation where the knife almost heals the blood flow, and the pictures were *marvelous*.

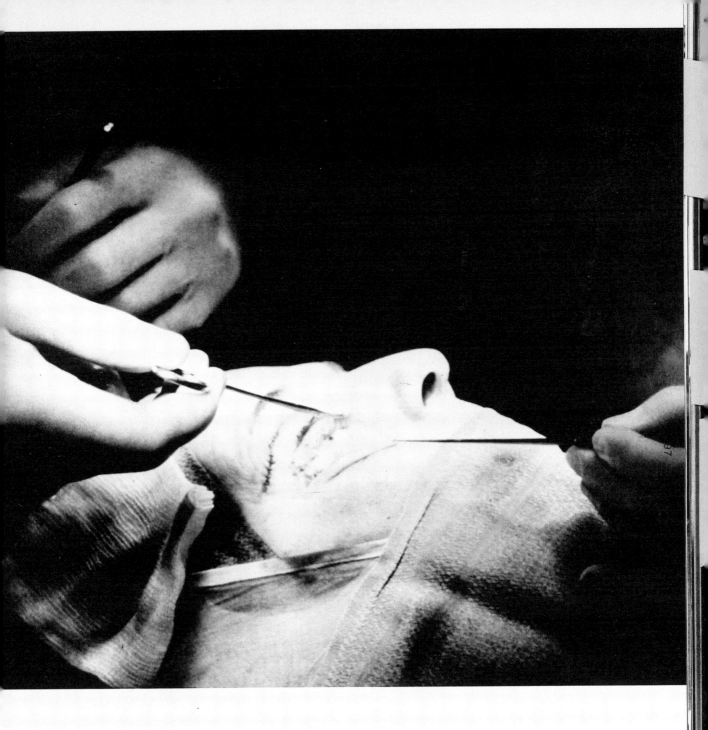

ELLIOTT ERWITT/MAGNUM
An eye-lift operation, 1960s

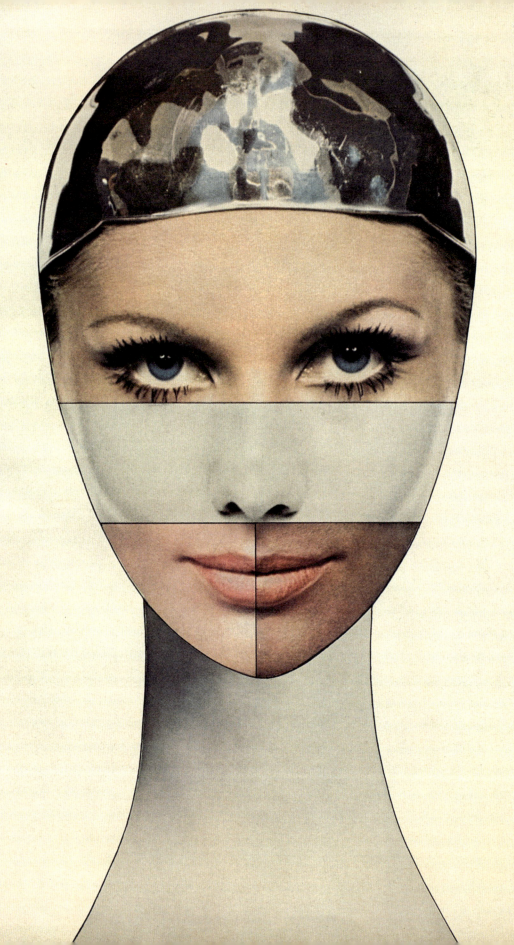

HAS CHANGED HER SHAPE

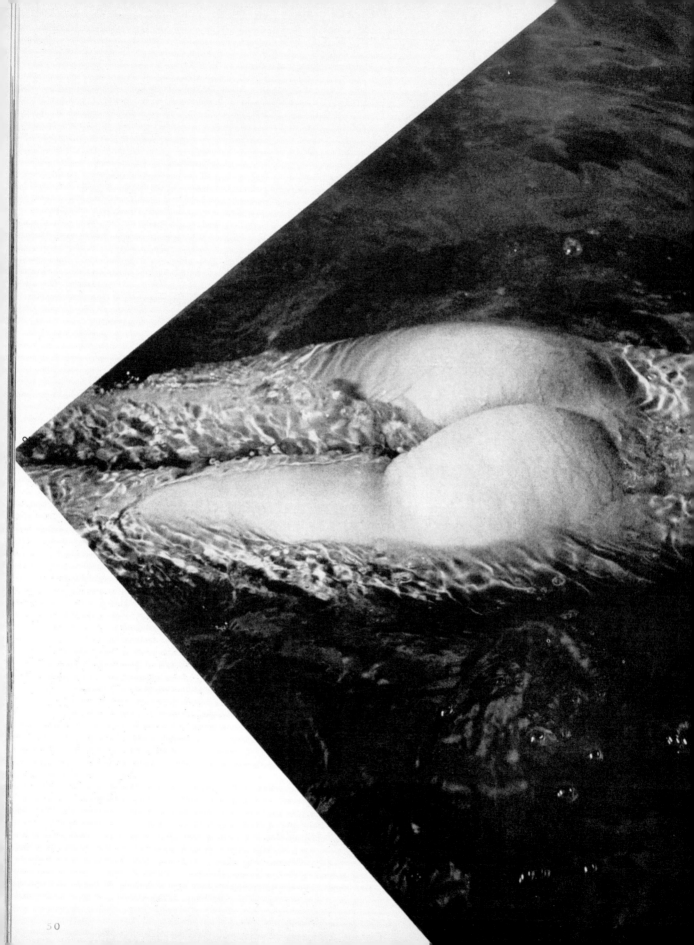

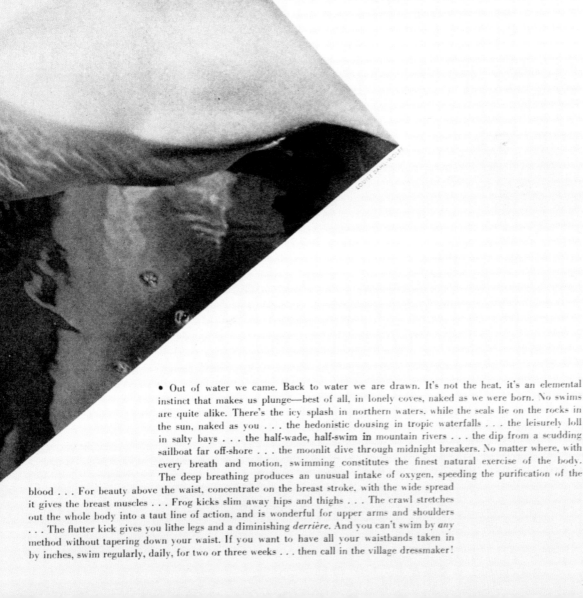

In Your Element

• Out of water we came. Back to water we are drawn. It's not the heat, it's an elemental instinct that makes us plunge—best of all, in lonely coves, naked as we were born. No swims are quite alike. There's the icy splash in northern waters, while the seals lie on the rocks in the sun, naked as you . . . the hedonistic dousing in tropic waterfalls . . . the leisurely loll in salty bays . . . the half-wade, half-swim in mountain rivers . . . the dip from a scudding sailboat far off-shore . . . the moonlit dive through midnight breakers. No matter where, with every breath and motion, swimming constitutes the finest natural exercise of the body. The deep breathing produces an unusual intake of oxygen, speeding the purification of the blood . . . For beauty above the waist, concentrate on the breast stroke, with the wide spread it gives the breast muscles . . . Frog kicks slim away hips and thighs . . . The crawl stretches out the whole body into a taut line of action, and is wonderful for upper arms and shoulders . . . The flutter kick gives you lithe legs and a diminishing *derrière*. And you can't swim by *any* method without tapering down your waist. If you want to have all your waistbands taken in by inches, swim regularly, daily, for two or three weeks . . . then call in the village dressmaker!

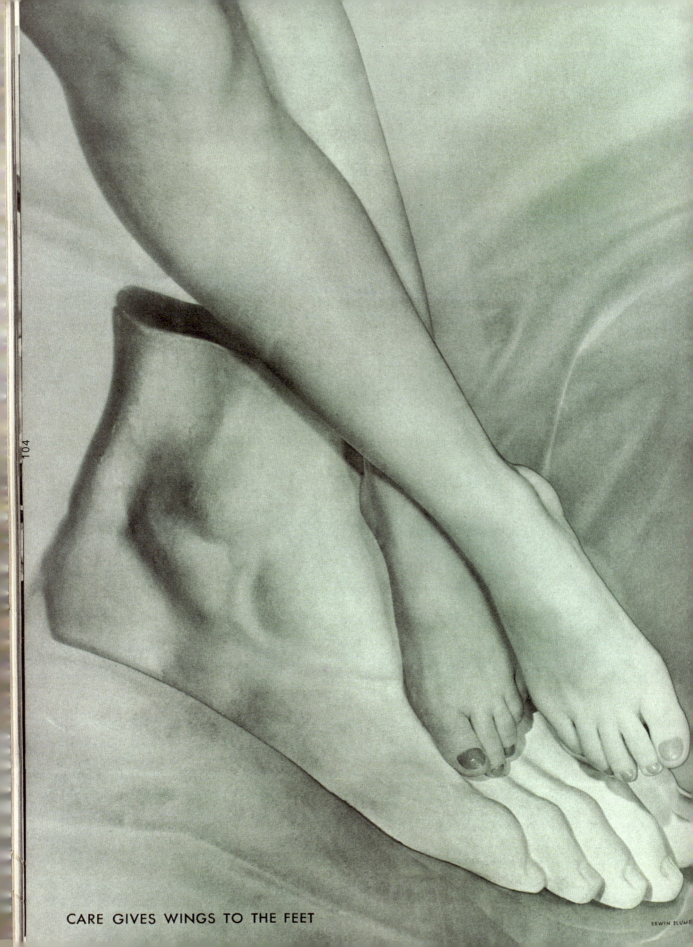

104

CARE GIVES WINGS TO THE FEET

ERWIN BLUME

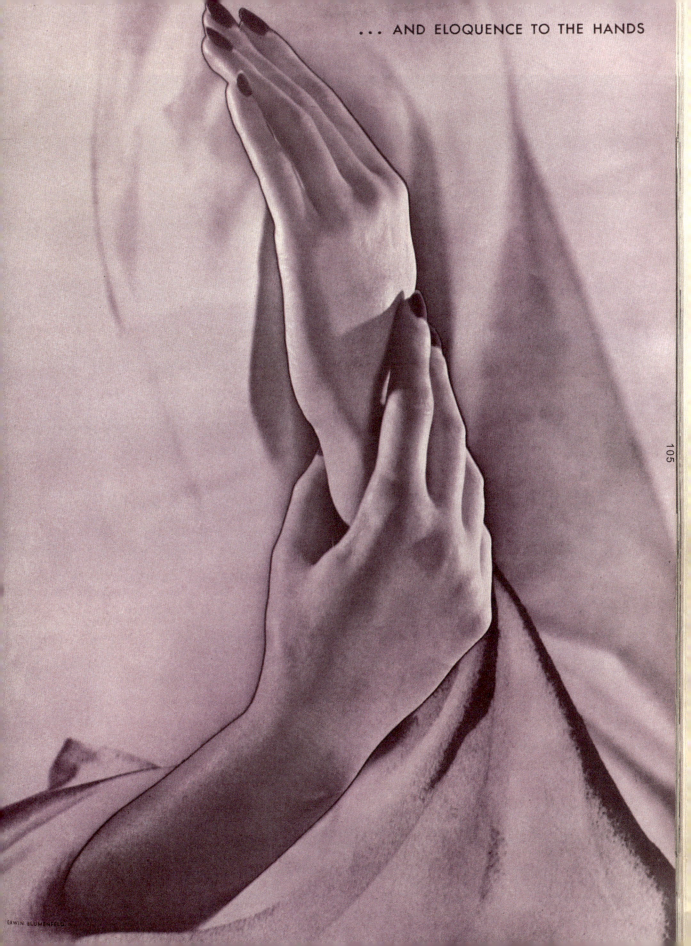

ERWIN BLUMENFELD

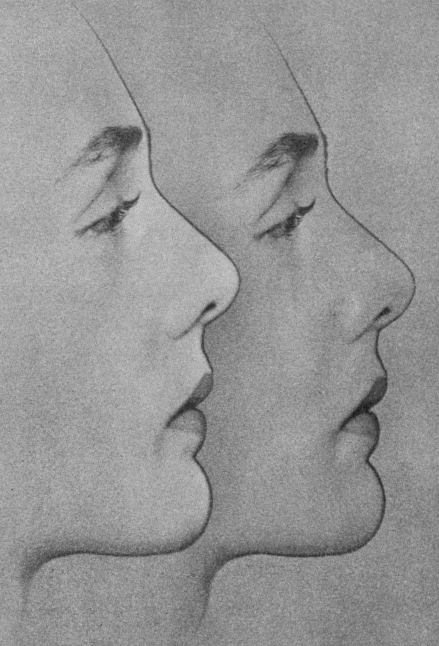

middle shade. Sometime in December you will shift to the paler glow. Back again in April to the middle shade. And once more in July to the darkest tint. No definite rules can be given, since California light is not New York light, and since you may break your winter by a trip South. You will have to watch the effect of light on the skin as an artist does. The sunlight has a spectroscopic range that varies from blue to orange, depending on the intensity of its component parts. Once you train your eye to perceive the quality of light and its effect on colors and people, you can handle make-up with marvelous effect. You do not have to be a one-season beauty—on in summer, off in winter. You do not have to be pale beside your friend just back from Nassau. You do not have to look as wan as you feel after a siege of the flu. If you know you are at your best in the golden season, you can retain that glow the whole year round.

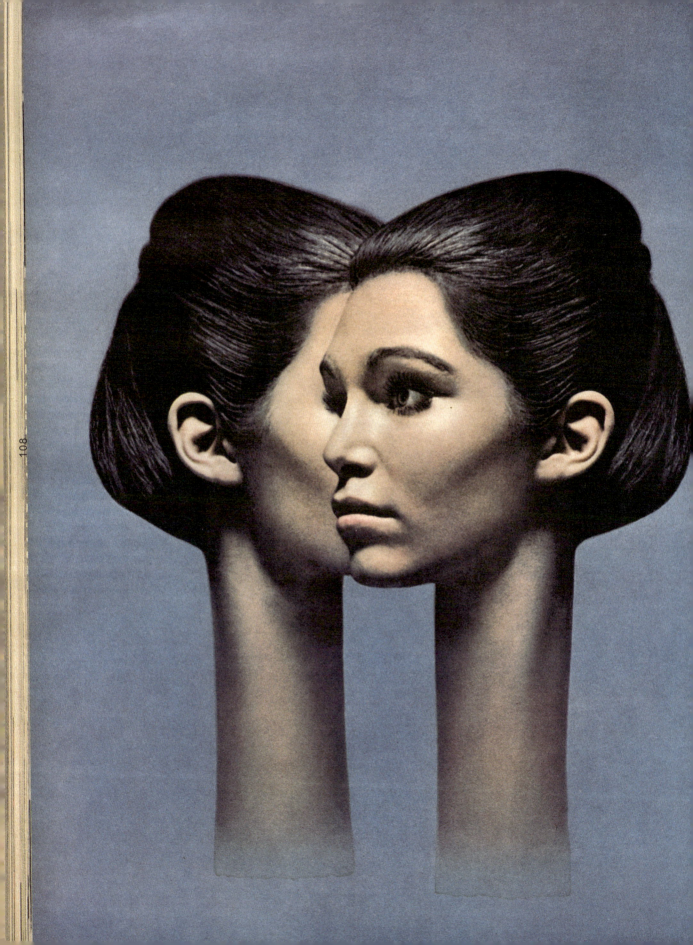

LESLIE GILL

1

2

wa
se
he
Fa
id
lo
si
li
hi
of
ca
"E

BAZA

CHÉR

Square-tipped fingernails and the profile of a young Cleopatra—the twenty-year-old Nile-queen of rock, at left, a girl who knows how to flesh fantasy into full-tilt fascination....There are the geometric fingernails, first of all. And the geometric hair—a straight, thick, shining black banner, smooth as a seal's coat over the small, perfect oval head, triangled at the finish line; the point resting seductively in the curve of her back....There are the blunt little cat's-whisker side-burns, and the dark droop of bangs in which she cuts two circumflexes—the better to see those burning-coal eyes with their extravagant freight of lashes and liners and shadows, impeccably applied, often without a mirror...she knows her looks that well. Knows how to use them. Does.

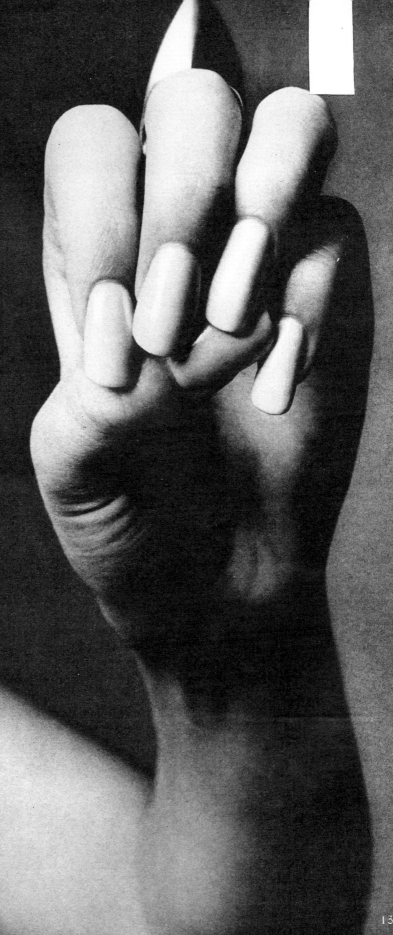

AVEDON

→

uffs,
and
me.

ROME
KACSI

'S BAZAAR

Mrs. JOHN F. KENNEDY—BEAUTY RADIANT WITH HEART AND SPI

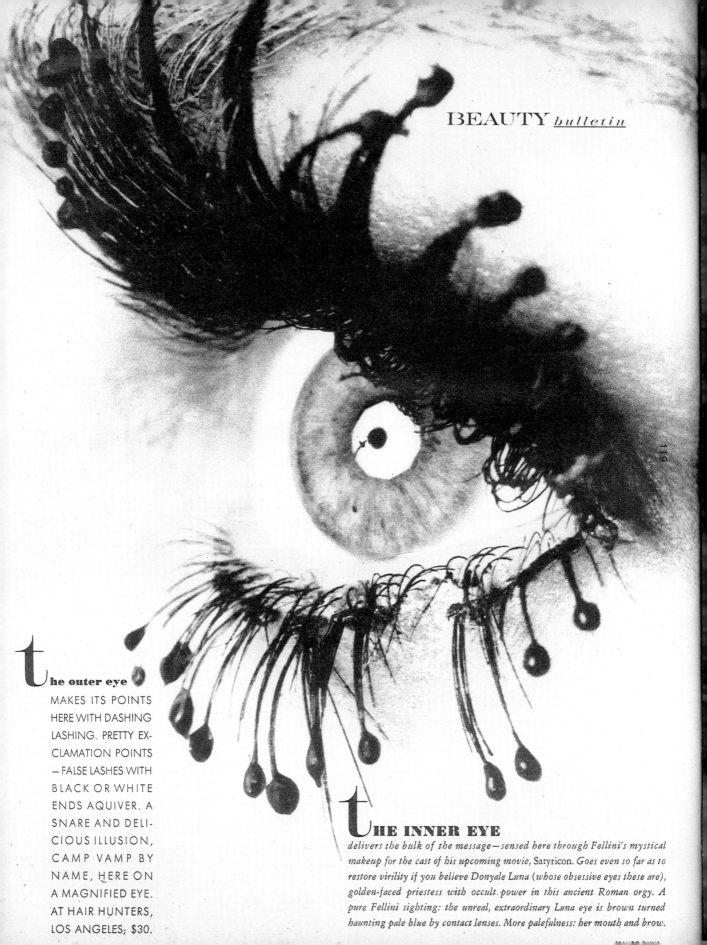

The outer eye

MAKES ITS POINTS HERE WITH DASHING LASHING. PRETTY EX-CLAMATION POINTS — FALSE LASHES WITH BLACK OR WHITE ENDS AQUIVER. A SNARE AND DELICIOUS ILLUSION, CAMP VAMP BY NAME, HERE ON A MAGNIFIED EYE. AT HAIR HUNTERS, LOS ANGELES; $30.

The inner eye

delivers the bulk of the message—sensed here through Fellini's mystical makeup for the cast of his upcoming movie, Satyricon. Goes even so far as to restore virility if you believe Donyale Luna (whose obsessive eyes these are), golden-faced priestess with occult power in this ancient Roman orgy. A pure Fellini sighting: the unreal, extraordinary Luna eye is brown turned haunting pale blue by contact lenses. More palefulness: her mouth and brow.

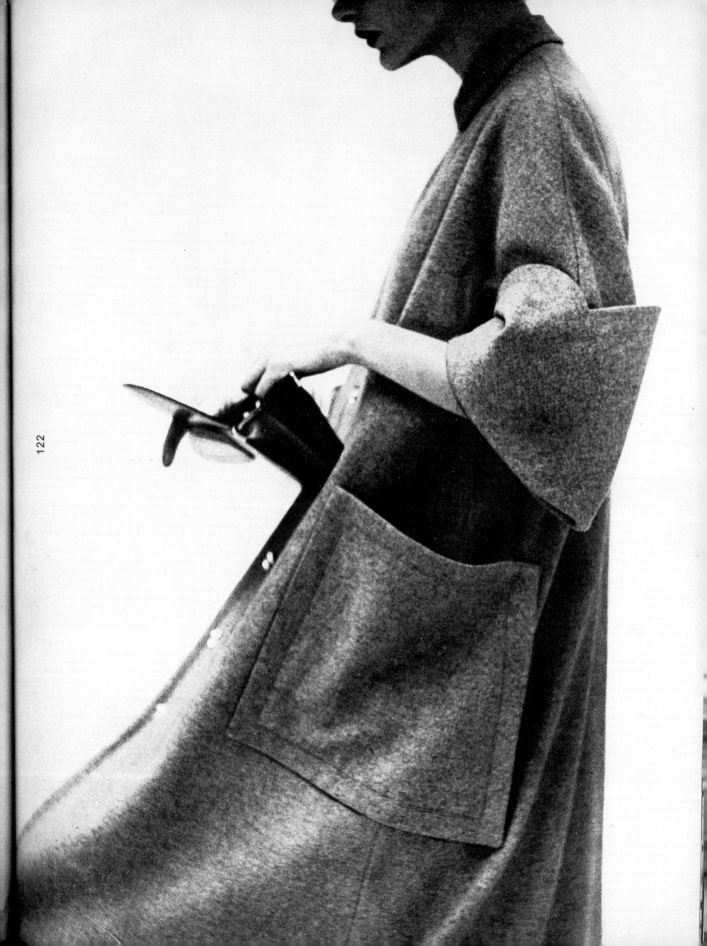

This thing

Pizazz, to quote the editor of the Harvard *Lampoon*, is an indefinable dynamic quality, the *je ne sais quoi* of function; as, for instance, adding Scotch puts the pizazz into a drink. Certain clothes have it, too. 1. There's pizazz in this rust evening coat, swinging wide in back, jutting crazily over the shoulders, clasped with a cord at the throat. Philippe et Gaston at Chez Ninon. 2. And in the pigskin vanity. Using gamy leather for a

called

woman's frailties has great tang. Koret. Bonwit Teller. Marshall Field, Chicago. Scarf from Guillemin of Paris.
3. A faille jacket from Charlie James' dynamic collection can spike up all your clothes — briefly, brilliantly.
4. A fur sweater in summer ermine, ocelot, or any sleek flat fur zipped close will put the pizazz into tramping and driving. Saks Fifth Avenue, New York and Chicago.
5. Beige, the color of the season, alights on the jackets of countless suits. Here it's in wool, with a black twill skirt, a frilled beige blouse. Bergdorf Goodman has it.
6. Spice in the white stitching of a Nat Lewis calf envelope. In the fringe of Guillemin's scarf. In the slit of Kislav's glove gored up the back. Best. Marshall Field, Chicago.
7. Spring boutonnieres of field flowers for your gray flannel suit. They are Neva-wetted against the April showers and won't bow down to water. Altman has them.
8. Beige again. Gabrielle's beige linen jacket buttoned with bright brass over a navy linen dress. Excitement for the first spring week-ends. Both from Chez Ninon.
9. Startling as the word pizazz itself, Gabrielle's jacket of purple and yellow silk, lined with purple wool jersey, will cause astonishment with any dress. Chez Ninon.

I loved my clothes from Chanel. [...] If you could have seen my clothes from Chanel in the thirties—the *dégagé* gypsy skirts, the divine brocades, the little boleros, the roses in the hair, the pailletted nose *veils*—day and evening! And the ribbons were so pretty.

I have a passion for armor. To me, a gauntlet is the most beautiful thing. The golden fingers, the wrist line. I always have armor in my Metropolitan shows. You don't notice them? In "Vanity Fair" I had a very beautiful lace room, and in the middle of it I had a gold breastplate. In was swollen gold... and out of the neck poured *point de Bruxelles*, the most beautiful lace in the world. The combination of gold and steel and lace!—no combination as beautiful.

Oh, I'm mad about armor. *Mad* about it! I love the way it's put together. I love the helmets with the feathers out the back. Milanese, you see.

But what Elsie Mendl had was something else that's particularly American—an appreciation of vulgarity. Vulgarity is a very important ingredient in life. I'm a great believer in vulgarity—if it's got vitality. A little bad taste is like a nice splash of paprika. We all need a splash of bad taste—it's hearty, it's healthy, it's physical. I think we could use *more* of it. *No* taste is what I'm against.

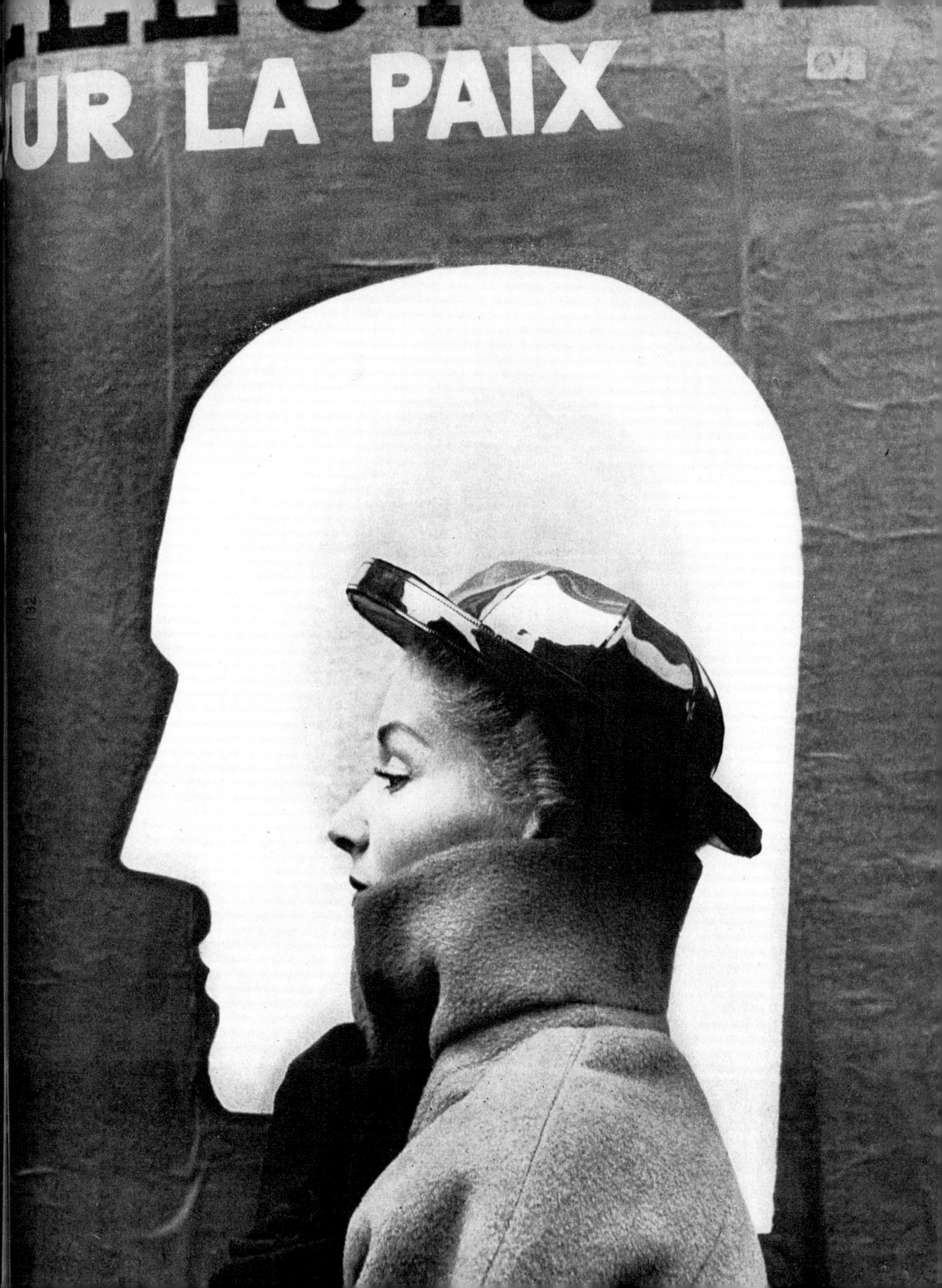
UR LA PAIX

HERBERT MATTER

The Woman Who Lost Her Head

• This woman is the national nightmare. At the first scent of victory

she walks out on her war job, walks into the shops. She buys by the dozen, yawns at inflation,

thinks she's pretty coony to stock up while the going is good.

Multiplied by the thousands, she is draining the shops, cornering merchandise needed by others, shooting

up prices, paving the way for postwar breadlines. She is the disgrace,

the despair of America—this hit and run shopper, this selfish, complacent little woman who has lost her head.

Pin-ups in Pants...

The boys pin up the girls, and the girls pin up Frank Sinatra.

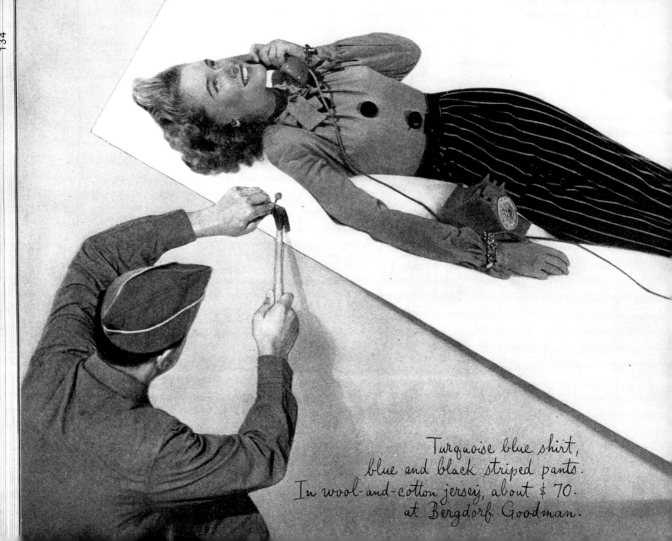

Turquoise blue shirt, blue and black striped pants. In wool-and-cotton jersey, about $70. at Bergdorf Goodman.

Slacks and shirts
stepped up with jewels
and the scent of
Frances Denney's "Night Life."
Right: Shocking pink shirt,
purple pants. In wool
jersey, about $55.
By Rose Barrack.
Bergdorf Goodman.

ERWIN BLUMENFELD

But where do you begin? The first thing to do, my love, is to arrange to be born in Paris. [...] After that, everything follows quite naturally.

During this phase when I lived in Albany I'd walk around in a mackintosh and a *béret basque* with *very* extreme, very exaggerated makeup—I've always had a strong Kabuki streak. I'd be criticized, but Lulu Van Rensselaer adored it.

I never wore clothe from Seventh Avenue myself, you understand. I always kept a totally European view of things. Maybe that's why I was so appreciated there. I was independent.

Fashion is a passing thing—a thing of fancy, fantasy, and feeling. Elegance is innate. It has nothing to do with being well-dressed. It's a quality possessed by certain thoughts and certain animals. Gazelles, I suppose, have elegance with their tiny heads and their satiny coats and their little winning ways. Gazelle have elegance. And Audrey Hepburn— magnificently. Elegance is refusal.

My Love—A coiffure
brushed smoothly from a diagonal
part into wide cherubic curls.
Designed by Maxime of Elizabeth Arden
to celebrate her new perfume, "My Love." The make-up is
keyed to Elizabeth Arden's new lipstick and nail enamel shade, "Blush Rose."

KODACHROME BY ERNST BEADLE

96

A WORLD'S FAIR IN THE WORKS, AND
THE CLOTHES THAT GET WITH IT —

IDEA

It's a dashing idea for spring in the city—suits
and coats with new walking skirts: wider-
hemmed, young, free, swinging, and—above all
—short. What these clothes will dash to, starting
April 22: an exciting show of dinosaurs (one
poses, toothily, at the left) featured by Sinclair,
IBM's oval theatre that sucks up banks of people to show them the think-ways of computers,
Alaska's iglooful of northern lights, and all the
other wonders in the square mile of New York
that's getting ready to be the 1964 World's Fair.
The short walking skirt, left, slanted to fullness
and part of a chalk-white suit, entering here on
the arm of a dinosaur who's prepared to lecture,
in an appropriate setting, about his own life
and times. Other suit-facts: a cropped cardigan,
overblouse of navy-blue dots. Suit by Stephan,
of Narco rayon (Jacques Maisch fabric); about
$55 at Saks Fifth Avenue; Halle Bros.; Neu-
steters. White kidskin hat by Halston, to order
at Bergdorf Goodman. Shoes by Herbert Levine.
Pink in a walk, right, a suit with pleat-eased
skirt, the shorter wider hem that's news now.
Under the tabbed jacket, a sleeveless pink overblouse. By Marquise, of Fibranne; about $245
at Lord & Taylor; Blum's, Chicago; Harold's.
Hat by Emme. Both pages: Van Raalte gloves.

WIDER-HEMMED, SHORTER,
ALL MADE FOR WALKING

HARPER'S BAZAAR

PRESENTS

AUDREY HEPBURN
MEL FERRER
PARIS PURSUIT

A LOVE FARCE

FEATURING THE PARIS COLLECTIONS

WITH BUSTER KEATON   DIRECTED BY RICHARD AVEDON

PLUS THE AMERICAN FASHION OPENINGS

SEPTEMBER 1959
60 CENTS

SCENE: MOULIN ROUGE, SAME NIGHT

1st COCOTTE: (speaking to Thunderbrow)
Je m'excuse, Monsieur,
but here they do not
serve la Prairie Oyster!

2nd COCOTTE: Why do you go on
speaking of this one girl
with her eyes! Come
along, bébé, we'll show
you eyes—and lips—
and legs. We'll show you
le vrai Paris!

Asymmetrical evening décolletage (right): Nina Ricci's slender, fluid column of crimson Shantung satin is drawn over one shoulder in soft folds and clasped by a giant rose, leaving the other shoulder bare. Floor-length dress, in Staron's silk.

Longer waist, shorter evening skirt (opposite): Heim's white dress of ruched ribbon lace is marked off in black at a deep-set midriff, an above-ankle hemline. Marescot lace of Du Pont nylon. At Macy's. Carven's Vert et Blanc perfume.

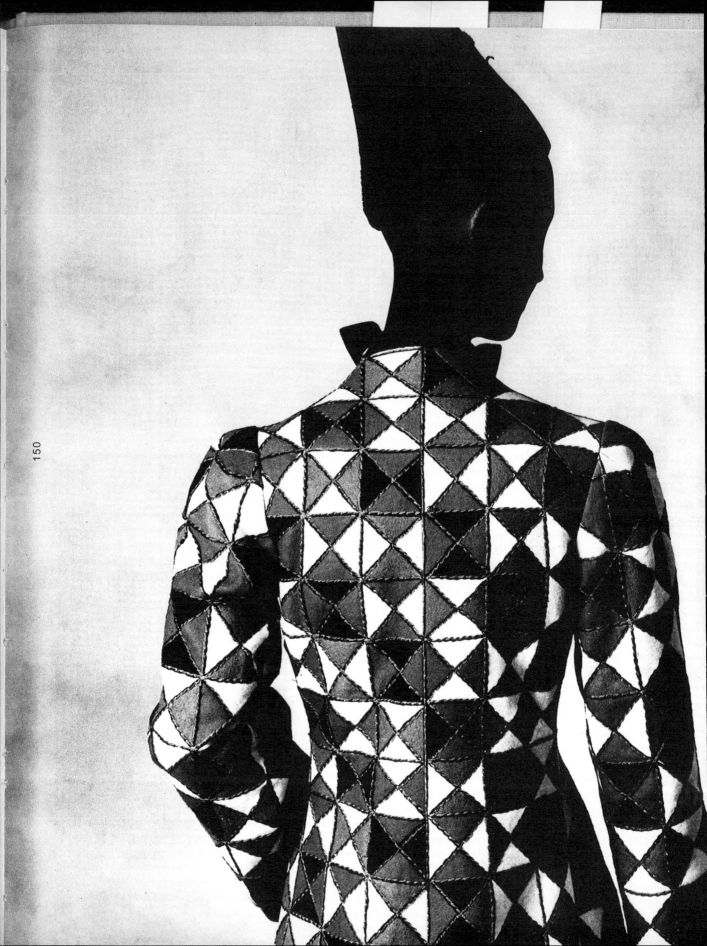

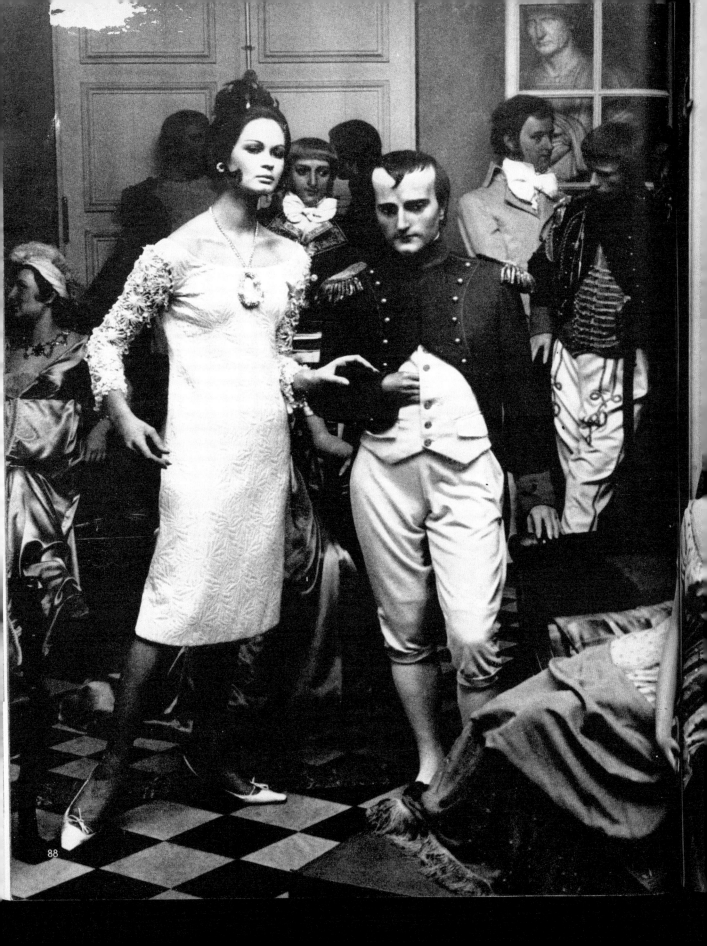

I don't think anyone has ever been in a better place at a better time than I was when I was editor of *Vogue*. *Vogue* always did stand for people's lives. I mean, a new dress doesn't get you anywhere; it's the life you're living in the dress, and the sort of life you had lived before, and what you will do in it later. Like all great times, the sixties were about personalities. It was the first time when mannequins *became* personalities. It was a time of great goals, an *inventive* time... and these girls invented *themselves*. Naturally, as an editor I was there to help them along.

At the same time mannequins became personalities in the sixties, personalities became mannequins. It was my idea to use Barbra Streisand as a mannequin. Her success was *overnight*. I sent her to Paris with Dick Avedon to model the collections. We sent her twice. We shot her in profile with that Nefertiti nose of hers... the pictures were awfully chic.

Today only personality counts [...] ravishing personalities are the most riveting things in the world — conversation, people's interests, the atmosphere that they create round them — these are the things that I feel are the only things worth putting in any issue.

I think stars are the only thing we have. We have a star, we follow a star... we may throw the star out tomorrow, but *today*, without a star, we wouldn't move at all.

Mainbocher's tawny paisley surah,
a long, back-flowing shimmer of taupe and umber
illuminations, turning golden in
the evening light. Over squarely strapped
shoulders, a little even, flat-collared jacket,
its edge dipped in brown mink.
Diamond and pearl earrings from Cartier.

Mainbocher's millefleurs shantung dinner
dress: its pinks, purples, green and gray
hazing together like a summer garden at twilight:
its small sleeves and dipping décolletage
buttoned under a periwinkle blue cashmere sweater—
a happy, effortless perfection. Kislav
glovelets; Mademoiselle pumps; Cartier diamonds.

RICHARD AVEDON

underskirt, and two floating panels that can

be twisted into a stole.

By Irene, in Ducharne fabric. Bergdorf Goodman; Frederick and Nelson; Neiman-Marcus.

seven
eight
nine
ten
eleven
XII
13

caviar

andy Warhol

Diana Vreeland on horse mannequin, early 1940s,
photographer unknown

"HAVE I EVER TOLD YOU ABOUT MY OBSESSION WITH HORSES?"

My grandmother had a huge farm horse in the country outside Katonah, New York, who wasn't used a great deal. He just stood in his stall. After lunch I'd run off, get on the horse. I had to use steps because he was enormous, *and I'd sit there all afternoon, perfectly happy. It would get hot, the flies would buzz . . . occasionally he'd swat his tail because the flies were bothering him, and I'd just sit there. That's all I wanted—just to be with the* steam *and the* smell *of that divine horse. Horses smell much better than people— I can tell you that.*

I was almost intuitive about horses. I can remember standing on the corner of Seventy-ninth Street and Park Avenue. I'd suddenly say, "Horse, horse, horse!"—and a horse would come around the corner! Naturally, my fixation was practically over by then, but I could smell the oats and the hay coming around the corner.

D.V. by Diana Vreeland,
ed. by George Plimpton and Christopher Hemphill,
Alfred A. Knopf, New York, 1984, pp. 20–21.

160

KODACHROME BY LOUISE DAHL-WOLFE

Mrs. Millicent Rogers emphasizes the chic of a perfect white linen blouse, full-blown and fresh as a great white rose. By Valentina. Under the collar she has tied a cowboy kerchief of orchid silk. On her nails the bright accent of Revlon's "Sweet Talk" nail polish. Her jewelry is a fascinating mixture: The Russian order of St. Catherine in huge diamonds, a modern diamond ring, a silver and coral necklace, Navajo bracelets picked up on her recent visit to New Mexico, and three gold rings which she made herself. For other examples of her skill as a goldsmith, see page 200.

BAZAAR

ULL
EPORT
N
ARIS-
MERICAN
OLLECTIONS

ETTERS
F
. H. LAWRENCE

EPTEMBER 1961
0 CENTS

171

VOGUE

75c
APR.15

FASHIONS THAT MAKE YOUR BEST SUMMER LOOKS

THE PILL— AND MORE
LATEST EXPERIMENTS IN BIRTH CONTROL

BEAUTY
WHAT TO DO WHEN YOUR LOOKS GO WRONG

TAYLOR AND BURTON ON LOCATION

TRUMAN CAPOTE'S PRIVATE LOG

BALENCIAGA, GIVENCHY, MAINBOCHER

173

I adore artifice. I always have. I remember when I was thirteen or fourteen buying red lacquer in Chinatown for my fingernails. "What is that?" my mother said. "Where did you get it? Why did you get it?"

"Because," I said, "I want to be a Chinese princess." [...] Then... when I'd started going out a few years later, I discovered calcimine. If I was going out—and I went out almost every night—two and a half hours before my escort arrived I'd start with this huge bottle of calcimine (I forget the brand, but it was theatrical stuff)—a sponge... and I'd be totally calcimined from the waist up, out along the arms, the back, the neck, the throat, et cetera, et cetera. I had to do this alone, because my family didn't take much interest in what I was doing. Then, when my escort and I would get up to dance, he, in his black dinner jacket, would be totally white. I would come off on him. But he'd have to put up with it. It meant nothing to me—I looked like a lily!

Visual Data

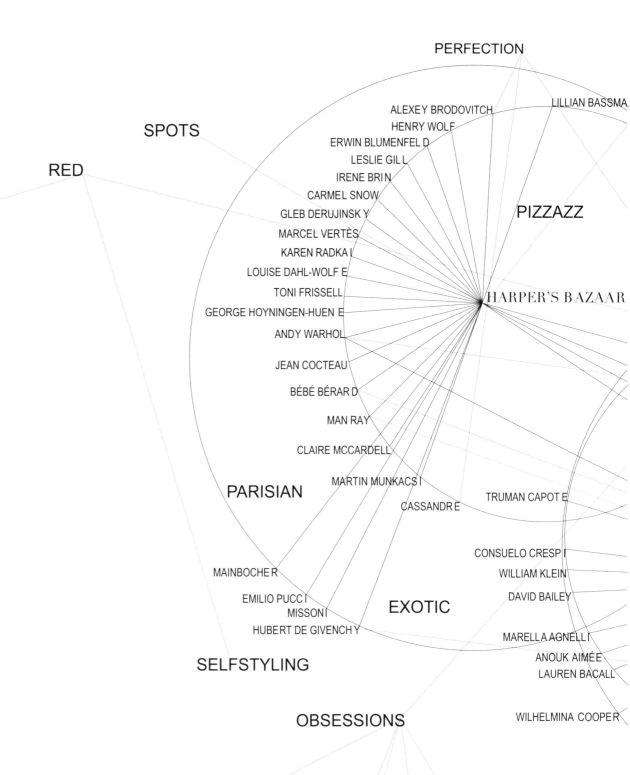

PERFECTION

SPOTS

RED

LILLIAN BASSMAN

ALEXEY BRODOVITCH
HENRY WOLF
ERWIN BLUMENFELD
LESLIE GILL
IRENE BRIN
CARMEL SNOW
GLEB DERUJINSKY
MARCEL VERTÈS
KAREN RADKAI
LOUISE DAHL-WOLFE
TONI FRISSELL
GEORGE HOYNINGEN-HUENE
ANDY WARHOL

PIZZAZZ

HARPER'S BAZAAR

JEAN COCTEAU

BÉBÉ BÉRARD

MAN RAY

CLAIRE MCCARDELL

MARTIN MUNKACSI

PARISIAN

CASSANDRE

TRUMAN CAPOTE

CONSUELO CRESPI

WILLIAM KLEIN

DAVID BAILEY

MAINBOCHER

EMILIO PUCCI
MISSONI
HUBERT DE GIVENCHY

EXOTIC

MARELLA AGNELLI

ANOUK AIMÉE
LAUREN BACALL

SELFSTYLING

WILHELMINA COOPER

OBSESSIONS

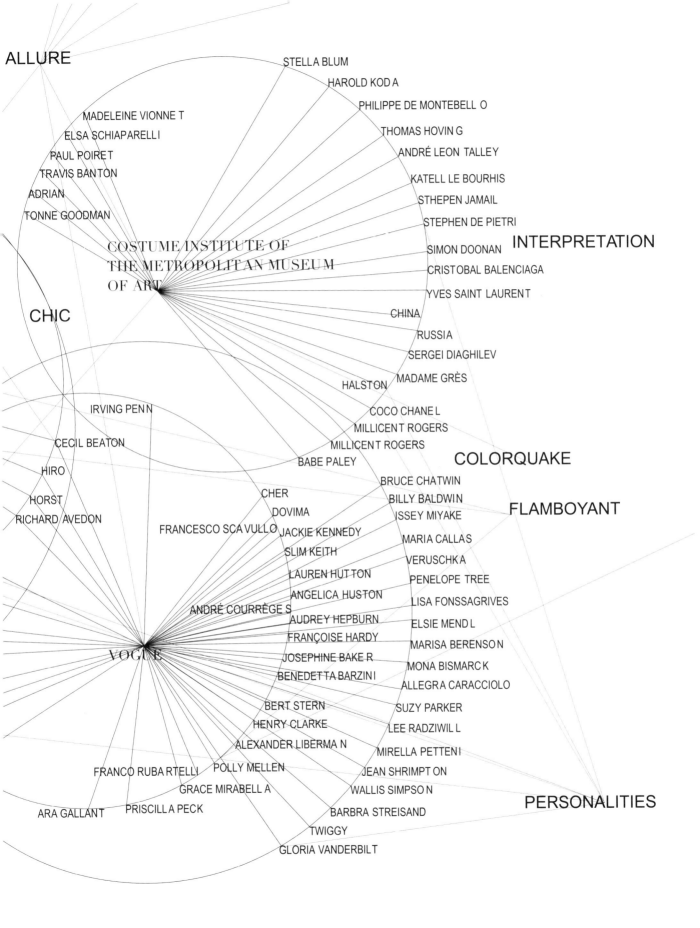

ALLURE

MADELEINE VIONNE T
ELSA SCHIAPARELLI
PAUL POIRET
TRAVIS BANTON
ADRIAN
TONNE GOODMAN

COSTUME INSTITUTE OF
THE METROPOLITAN MUSEUM
OF ART

STELLA BLUM
HAROLD KOD A
PHILIPPE DE MONTEBELL O
THOMAS HOVIN G
ANDRÉ LEON TALLEY
KATELL LE BOURHIS
STHEPEN JAMAIL
STEPHEN DE PIETRI
SIMON DOONAN
CRISTOBAL BALENCIAGA
YVES SAINT LAURENT

INTERPRETATION

CHIC

IRVING PENN

CECIL BEATON

HIRO

HORST
RICHARD AVEDON

FRANCESCO SCAVULLO

CHER
DOVIMA
JACKIE KENNEDY
SLIM KEITH
LAUREN HUTTON
ANGELICA HUSTON
ANDRÉ COURRÈGE S
AUDREY HEPBURN
FRANÇOISE HARDY
JOSEPHINE BAKE R
BENEDETTA BARZINI

VOGUE

CHINA
RUSSIA
SERGEI DIAGHILEV
MADAME GRÈS
HALSTON
COCO CHANEL
MILLICENT ROGERS
MILLICENT ROGERS
BABE PALEY

COLORQUAKE

BRUCE CHATWIN
BILLY BALDWIN
ISSEY MIYAKE

FLAMBOYANT

MARIA CALLAS
VERUSCHKA
PENELOPE TREE
LISA FONSSAGRIVES
ELSIE MENDL
MARISA BERENSO N
MONA BISMARC K
ALLEGRA CARACCIOLO
SUZY PARKER
LEE RADZIWIL L
MIRELLA PETTEN I
JEAN SHRIMPT ON
WALLIS SIMPSO N
BARBRA STREISAND
TWIGGY
GLORIA VANDERBILT

BERT STERN
HENRY CLARKE
ALEXANDER LIBERMA N
POLLY MELLEN
FRANCO RUBA RTELLI
GRACE MIRABELL A
ARA GALLANT
PRISCILLA PECK

PERSONALITIES

Where to Put the Ideas. Re-Curating Diana Vreeland

Mrs Vreeland often emphasized that we were only re-editing other people's editing, but in our reworking of the material, it became our own.

The picture I'm looking for may never have existed.
DV

And I'm terrible on facts. But I always have an idea. If you have an idea, you're well ahead.
DV

The question raised when curating an exhibition of the work (and life) of Diana Vreeland, and more importantly when designing it, is where to put the ideas, or rather what kind of interpretation suits her work. I have long been a defender of Diana Vreeland, working within the world, not of fashion magazines, but of the museum, and my position has been mainly a sort of stubborn reaction to British dress historians whose criticism of Vreeland is often joyless. My interest begins at the end of her life when she was special consultant within the Costume Institute and so with what is now considered her curatorial work. In brief, her attitude to dramatically styled fashion that created iconic double-page spreads for *Harper's Bazaar* and *Vogue* was criticized as anachronistic frivolity

when applied to historic costume within a museum setting by dress historians who believed this corrupted the ability for dresses to clearly and accurately represent the age in which they had been created[1].

As an exhibition-maker and not a dress historian I have a perspective that is perhaps new in relation to Diana Vreeland, which is that I take her mannequin gestures, her abstracted heads, her huge props, her music, her perfumed halls just as seriously as I take her well documented "mis"-accessorizing of the gowns and the verisimilitude of the historical "look." I have in fact been seduced by her audacity to take nothing as given however old it might be, within what was a very narrow vocabulary and in many ways still seems so today.

Diana Vreeland After Diana Vreeland wants to imitate Vreeland, to work in the manner of, as though mimicking a school of art, and to see what we might make of her now—now that so much of her curatorial idiom is seen in museums everywhere. It has been difficult to make anything in fact look very different or new within this exhibition such has been the pervasive use of her distinctive style within museum displays worldwide. Now that fashion exhibitions have become blockbuster spectacles, and it is no longer exceptional for a living designer to have a show, it is more interesting than ever before to look at what Vreeland was doing. Now, when the shock of her work has been absorbed, to design an exhibition of her work is to exercise restraint not excess.

Representing her—commissioning wigs, plinths, mannequins and props, wanting to try to get her "look" right—takes us back to square one. Curatorial theory is now too established, too academic for us to act unintentionally, and the question might now be, how intentionally was she acting? How much precision was there in her creative delirium?

Diana Vreeland provoked a discipline to collide with its limits. Dress historians and curators were asked to address the difference between what was considered until then "neutral" historicized display (however disingenuous) and over-interpretation, or worse over-styling which is not a risk that other arts run. Within art criticism there was (certainly until recently) a conviction as to where the limits of the work of art were. Usually somewhere around the frame. Dress is always incomplete. It is always asking of the curator to complete it, with a surrogate body, a head, arms and legs that emerge from the dress. It is interesting

to consider (within dress) what might dilute or corrupt a silhouette. In 2000 Robert Wilson took the question to its extreme with La Rosa perfectly crafted "invisible" mannequins for the Armani retrospective at the Guggenheim—nothing visible other than the dress. As visitors we completed the mannequins in our contemporary minds; I am convinced that we edited out the 1970s styling that accompanied some of the outfits in their initial design—so why was Vreeland literally completing the dress according to contemporary fashionable criteria so disturbing?

For the purpose of this exhibition, the question is how does her distinctive if controversial voice come through in the presentation of objects: both in their selection and how they are staged; an exhibition that has to contain within in it the 12 exhibitions that Vreeland curated at the Met. Re-created exhibitions is a concept rehearsed and debated within the art world, but never in the world of dress history, and it is strange that this discipline should have lagged so far behind. It has become a motif within a debate around a creative hierarchy between artist and curator, and curator as "maker." If the curator becomes an author then a whole exhibition might be quoted.

Diana Vreeland After Diana Vreeland has been hosted by the Musei Civici di Venezia at Palazzo Fortuny in association with the newly formed Diana Vreeland Estate established by Alexander Vreeland, her grandson, and his wife, Lisa. Mariano Fortuny's Venetian palace was chosen for its associations evocative of both the European aristocratic and cosmopolitan lives that Vreeland found irresistible, and Venice in its enigma: Venice as a gateway to the East and all its imaginative possibilities. The Venice of Venetian balls featured in Vreeland's society pages of Harper's Bazaar and Vogue and her love of Orientalist styling which is now famous, Veruschka's dramatic Japonisme or Turquerie. Venice has been chosen intentionally over London, New York or Paris in order to have an outsiders view.

Diana Vreeland loved Mariano Fortuny's designs, and styled his famous Grecian tea gowns that contained movement within them, and that she found so utterly modern in the pages of her magazines. She collected more Fortuny gowns for the Met than any other designer and there is something about their total environments that is similar, as well as their fearlessness about oriental decoration.
The Fortuny as a venue, has been associated for the last few years with the dramatic Biennale exhibitions of contemporary art that the director Daniela Ferretti and Axel Vervoordt have created where largely abstract art has been placed around the building as if to further furnish it, but has also hosted exhibitions of fashion houses Roberta di Camerino and Capucci, Diana Vreeland After Diana Vreeland occupies two floors of the palazzo, the "piano nobile," Fortuny's own luxuriously furnished salotto and the second floor: the first intimate, the second open and more public, the first looks at her origins and her formative passions, the second, at her work—and how those passions were styled and staged for audiences over almost fifty years.

Note
1   I have written about those years in an essay entitled "Re-styling History: DV at the Costume Institute," in Diana Vreeland: The Eye Has To Travel. New York: Harry N. Abrams, 2011, pp. 225-44, associated with this project commissioned and edited by Lisa Immordino Vreeland. Valerie Steele offers a very clear account of Diana Vreeland's work at the Metropolitan Museum and the controversy it created in her "Museum Quality. The Rise of the Fashion Exhibition," Fashion Theory: The Journal of Dress, Body & Culture, vol. 12, no. 1, 2008, pp. 7-30.

For years I couldn't get over Callas… DV

*The Ballets Russes, which is the only avant-garde
I've ever known…* DV

The exhibition is built on the idea of accumulation and
association rather than on the idea of linear chronology.
Tableaux that are evocative of a life, rather than its
retelling. The exhibition intentionally doesn't start with
graphic drama, blown up iconic Avedon or Louise Dahl-
Woolfe images that one might expect, to bring the
visitor in on a note of recognition, but instead it begins
with a cabinet with a suit of armor, a red cape worn
by Maria Callas and a red gown designed by Worth
(cabinet 1: "History"). The three objects are fundamental
to Vreeland, not because she owned them or indeed
ever saw them, but because they hold clues to what
she was looking for and clues to important strands
that ran through her life, both personally and eventually
professionally. As with Vreeland's work the exhibition
relies heavily on objects that represent her intersecting
passions. Just as her props added to the romance of her
shows at the Costume Institute, these objects illustrate
ideas about ritual, strength, power and couture. They are
all transformative objects; they transform people into

different roles and functions and places. That is what
Vreeland wanted dress to do, this is the demand that she
made on the material. These objects shun the everyday,
the bland, and the routine; and they introduce us to her
beloved reds and metallic palettes. These themes haunt
the rest of the exhibition.

The other cabinets within Fortuny's first floor lounge
leap forward in time, the second (cabinet 2: "Styling
History") to Leon Bakst's "Costume for a Bayadere,"
1912, a prelude to her love of the Orient, flanked by
two ensembles owned by Vreeland, one her favourite
pagoda-collared YSL suit which she donated to the
Metropolitan Museum of Art, and her pink and black
Valentino ensemble also adorned (if more simply) with a
pagoda collar. The Balles Russes, so loved by Vreeland
signified a real rupture for her, a daring break from
the Belle Époque monotone fashions she describes in
her autobiography, as well as a symbol of Modernity;
her excitement conveyed through descriptions of her
childhood which she claimed included visits to her home
by impresario Sergei Diaghilev himself, and Nijinsky. Her
own style, coming from her own history. From her early
experiences she not only appropriated decorative motifs
but worlds of imagined gestures, poses; of bodies

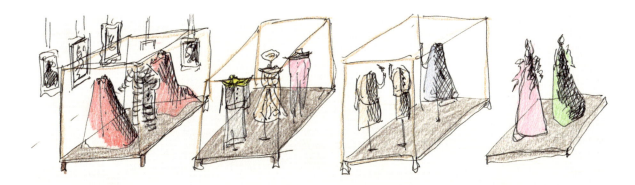

diagonally leaping through the air that seem to inform
her editorial flair. Bodies in movement, prepared for
movement, or poised for change.

The last cabinet (cabinet 3: "DV Style") in the salotto
is Vreeland herself: her uniform, her studied and
recognizable chic. Two almost identical Givenchy suits
and a Mainbocher coat accessorized by the mannequin's
arms: the arms cast as if she were smoking her
cigarettes in their long holders, which are as distinctive
as her aquiline nose or raven hair; she is posing as she
did when working or thinking. The bangles from Kenneth
Jay Lane adorned her arms as well as her mannequins.
She has been so often represented by illustrators and
caricaturists that her signature elements are immediately
recognizable: a waxwork model of her would be less like
"her" than a sketch. Behind the cabinet sit the famous
portraits of her lent by her family and friends, hung
from the layered hanging system of Fortuny's lounge in
front of his wallpaper and hanging fabrics, just as in her
cluttered home—they look as though they have always
been there. She has moved in.

The exhibition meanders through two further rooms on
the first floor that have been left unfurnished. The first
takes an intimate look at her family photographs, her

milieu; the second a different kind of milieu, one that she
chose—that of a young woman surrounded by people
staging fashion; fashion shows, couture clients being
recorded for the pages of magazines or posing for their
portraits. The protagonists of this room are Beaton,
Balenciaga and Mona Bismarck. Beaton's important and
eccentric compositions, his use of black and white, his
idea of using props for his aristocratic settings or the
gauze across the sitters face (that became Vreeland's
preferred mannequin styling). Beaton's sitters were
Balenciaga's clients and Diana Vreeland's friends. They
crystallized Vreeland's desire for a career in fashion.

Second Floor

The second floor of the Fortuny is dedicated to Diana
Vreeland's work beginning in 1936 at *Harper's Bazaar*.
Her idiom laid out across her double-page canvases
described and re-assembled in this catalog by Maria Luisa
Frisa, and her museum style are instantly recognizable.
The 12 cabinets do not represent the 12 exhibitions
that Diana Vreeland staged at the Metropolitan Museum
of Art between 1973 and 1984. Though they each
contain traces of her museum shows and their distinctive
styling—carry themes of her enduring fascinations that
wove in and out of her shows.

Diana Vreeland believed that all stories were dramatic. Her exhibitions at the Met had at the entrance a point of view, a vista, a prop! Usually a huge prop, here re-created by a horse. It is surrounded by three mannequins dressed in Pucci and Missoni, the Italian fashion houses she championed in America and whose color and glamour she so loved. The horse is no longer the 17th century white horse that she used in her first show, *The World of Balenciaga*, but its Italian counterpart that welcomes the visitor to Italy instead. Italy becomes our focal point, our point of view.

Her colors saturate the plinth and the mannequins, colors that ran through her exhibitions repeatedly, billiard table green, violet purple, "lavenders, orchids, or moonlit violets," and her signature red, … the red of any child's cap in a Renaissance painting. Her references are specific and vague. We all know what she means but we are not always sure exactly what she is referring to.

Balenciaga is a beginning, and Vreeland loved beginnings that were endlessly renewable. A retrospective of Balenciaga's magnificent work was her first show at the Met in 1973 when she exhibited the couture that had seduced her into fashion. She loved his ability to dedicate the room to the drama of one woman.

"I love nineteenth century colors. I love the names of colors of men's clothes of the Regency period — buff, sand, fawn... and don't forget snuff! My God, there were words in those days. Balenciaga had the most wonderful sense of color — his *tête de nègre*, his *café au lait*, his violets, his magentas, and his mauves. Every summer I'd take his same four pairs of slacks and his same four pullovers to Southampton with me. Then... one year I went down to Biarritz. I laid out exactly the same four pairs of slacks, exactly the same four pullovers... and I'd never seen them before! It's the light of course — the intensifying light of the Basque country. There's never been such a light. That was Balenciaga's country."
DV

Diana Vreeland adored uniforms.

Heads

Dear Mrs Vreeland,
I would like very much to work out a solution regarding the problem we have discussed with the presentation of mannequins. It is my opinion that the most sensible way of doing this is to utilize those which are already in possession of the museum. They could be covered with some sort of fabric which would eliminate the obvious identification problem—mannequins draped tautly with cloth or netting. [...]
I look forward to hearing from you regarding your opinion
Sincerely
Robert Mapplethorne

[Sept 8, 1972 in NYPL]

September 25 1972—from her letter to Stella Blum and Mavies Dalton.

Dear Stella and Mavies,
[...]
Re: Mannequins
It would be the most wonderful thing if you would send to

M. Robert Mapplethorne
[Address]

two heads from our mannequins as he would like to experiment with covering the features with pieces of cloth which might give an amusing effect in some cases of projecting fashion.

"As you know, one of my great worries is the whole mannequin situation as we don't want to look like Saks or Galleries Lafayette or the department store in any town or city in the world which is of course a great worry with all so-called life-like mannequins. Most life-like mannequins are rather creepy and unattractive and distract from the look of the dress."
DV

double net.

THE MANNEQUIN PROBLEM

I have used commissioned mannequins from the
historic Italian mannequin company La Rosa with
their recently developed half-abstract faces to style
the heads, nets, wigs and hats for the exhibition,
following Robert Mapplethorne's suggestion to Vreeland
of "covering the heads with 'tautly draped cloth.'"
Un-naturalistic color was Vreeland's other way of
abstracting mannequins from being too realistic and so
we have created her greens, reds, taxi-cab yellow and
violet as well as a dash of silver and gold.

Acclaimed fashion hair stylist Angelo Seminara has designed
wigs that link the worlds of fashion styling and of museum
staging, seeing "historic" wigs through contemporary eyes.
The 18th century wig created by Harold Koda when he
was an assistant to Vreeland is as iconic in its way as the
clothes she exhibited.

"Why don't you? Have a room done up in every color green? This will take months, years, to collect, but it will be delightful—a melange of plants, green glass, green porcelains, and furniture covered in sad greens, gay greens, clear, faded, and poison greens? And object across time where color coded 18th century and her coining of the phrase Palazzo Pyjama and her love of YSL are brought together because they are green, different greens. She privileged qualities of the object that may not be privileged today—the color over the 18th century?"
DV

There was always a green room in Vreeland's exhibitions.

"At *Harper's Bazaar* a story went around about me: Apparently I'd wanted a billiard-table green background for a picture. So the photographer went out and took the picture. I didn't like it. He went out and took it again. I didn't like it. Then... he went out and took it again and I still didn't like it. 'I asked for billiard-table green!' I'm supposed to have said. 'But this is a billiard table, Mrs Vreeland,' the photographer replied. 'My dear,' I apparently said, 'I meant the idea of billiard-table green, not a billiard table.'"
DV

Black and white
Africa
DV's mother's hunting trips
zebra
Le Chant du Rossignol
DV's zebra bangles
the black and white of the Belle Époque
ceremony
mourning
black Balenciaga…

The cabinet for Black and White is indebted to her double-page compositions and so the vertical structure of the cabinet uses a different set of rules: the cabinet frame becomes graphic lines across a page. The cabinet with its reference to fashion spreads disrupts the museum cabinet just as she disrupted the rules of museum practice with the rules of fashion.

Two shows that you cannot
always tell apart—Russia imagined by YSL (1983-84),
and historic Russia re-styled (1976-77).

The mannequin heads for the real historic Russian pieces
(lent by collector Martin Kamer) use the color Vreeland
preferred for fashion studio portraits.
The fashionable YSL ensembles are mounted on white
Shlappi mannequins. The YSL mannequins become a
dissonant anachronistic gesture in this exhibition to
suggest the "historic" touch.

"Taxi-cab yellow is marvellous. I often asked for
taxi-cab yellow backgrounds when I worked in
photography studios."
DV

Female Peasant's Holiday Dress
19th century. Vologda region.
121. SARAFAN Homespun primed linen. White-outlined vegetative
design worked with orange polka dots on a blue ground. Cut
straight and held up by narrow straps. Decorated with pieces of
calico and colored wool thread.
Inv. No. 57907 B-460. Acquired in 1920.
122. RUBAKHA Homespun linen canvas. Short. Embroidered in teal-
tinctured silk and flax worked in stem and darning stitches.
Inv. No. 14019 B-971. Acquired in 1972.

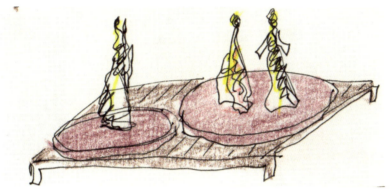

One of Vreeland's many orientalisms.

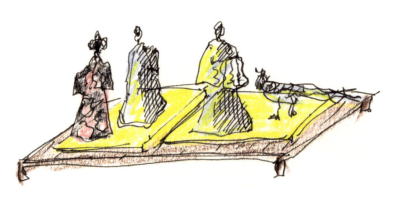

Japonisme and Chinoiserie are irreverently combined—
they recall two distinct exhibitions (*Diaghilev: Costumes
& Designs of The Ballets Russes*, December 20,
1978-April 15, 1979; *The Manchu Dragon: Costumes
of China—The Ch'ing Dinasty*, December 16,
1980-August 30, 1981; *La Belle Époque*, December 6,
1982-September 4, 1983), but combined in her pages
of *Vogue* as something fascinating and remote but not
specifically historical.

Couture from those years was the subject of Vreeland's exhibition but also represented for her a quintessential glamour and luxury. Chanel, Fortuny, and Schiaparelli. Her past and her preferences permeate all her exhibitions.

This tableau was one of the first that made a connection between dress and the art world explicitly, not so much by juxtaposing the dress with the Mondrian "original" on the wall, but by exhibiting it flat, on the wall—by treating it as art. It is about exhibition-making but she didn't call it that. By hanging a dress flat you are creating a different set of associations. Captions cannot do that work for us; she knew this intuitively.

Dalziel Curtains

"Why don't you, if you have a dark-dining room in a city apartment, stop trying to brighten it and paint in dark grape red and drape the windows in festoons of real Scotch tartan?"
DV

Vreeland was proud of her Scottish ancestry.
The Dalziels had not lived in Scotland for many generations but she loves their family motto: "I dare."

She wrote in her teenage diary: "I am Diana, a goddess, therefore ought to be wonderful, pure, marvelous, as only I alone can make myself... no one can ever rob me of that name, never shall I change it. Diana was a goddess and I must live up to that name,
Dalziel = I dare, therefore I dare, I dare change to day, and make myself exactly how I want to be."

Re-Viewing Vreeland Exhibitions

– THE WORLD OF BALENCIAGA, MARCH 23-SEPTEMBER 9, 1973 – THE 10S, THE 20S, THE 30S: INVENTIVE CLOTHES 1909-1939, DECEMBER 13, 1973-SEPTEMBER 3, 1974 – ROMANTIC AND GLAMOROUS HOLLYWOOD DESIGN, NOVEMBER 21, 1974-AUGUST 31, 1975 – AMERICAN WOMEN OF STYLE, DECEMBER 18, 1975-AUGUST 31, 1976 – THE GLORY OF RUSSIAN COSTUME, DECEMBER 9, 1976-SEPTEMBER 6, 1977 – VANITY FAIR: A TREASURE TROVE OF THE COSTUME INSTITUTE, DECEMBER 15, 1977-SEPTEMBER 3, 1978 – DIAGHILEV: COSTUMES & DESIGNS OF THE BALLETS RUSSES, DECEMBER 20,1978-APRIL 15, 1979 – FASHIONS OF THE HAPSBURG ERA: AUSTRIA-HUNGARY, DECEMBER 11, 1979-AUGUST 31, 1980 – THE MANCHU DRAGON: COSTUMES OF CHINA - THE CH'ING DYNASTY, DECEMBER 16, 1980-AUGUST 30, 1981 – THE EIGHTEENTH-CENTURY WOMAN, DECEMBER 16, 1981-SEPTEMBER 5, 1982 – LA BELLE ÉPOQUE, DECEMBER 6, 1982-SEPTEMBER 4, 1983 – YVES SAINT LAURENT, DECEMBER 6, 1983-SEPTEMBER 2,1984

Vreeland did not play a direct part in the preparation of the exhibitions that followed, but was involved in the formulation of the concept and through her staff:

– MAN AND THE HORSE, DECEMBER 18, 1984-SEPTEMBER 1, 1985 – THE COSTUMES OF ROYAL INDIA, DECEMBER 20, 1985-AUGUST 31, 1986 – DANCE, DECEMBER 17, 1986-SEPTEMBER 6, 1987

The play on words in the title *Re-Viewing Vreeland Exhibitions* is deliberate. The intention is to look at them again and appraise them. And looking back at the exhibitions that Diana Vreeland curated at the Costume Institute of the Metropolitan Museum of Art in New York during the period she held the post of special consultant (1972-89) is like passing in review what we can now consider common places and stereotypes of fashion. The exhibitions staged by Diana Vreeland identified modes like the celebratory retrospective devoted to the individual designer, or to a crucial moment in the evolution of Western fashion, such as the 18th century or the period of the avant-garde movements. They recognized the central role that personalities (the word Vreeland used for celebrities) have always played in the circulation of styles and in the construction of shared imagery. They anticipated the theme of the archives and permanent collection of a museum. They set trends and at the same time crystallized the obsessions that trigger processes in fashion design, such as Chinese and Indian orientalism or the precious and excessive atmospheres typical of the nobility. The exhibitions curated by Vreeland are places to which we periodically return and propose again: we are thinking of the exhibition *Diaghilev and the Golden Age of the Ballets Russes, 1909-1929* held at the Victoria and Albert Museum from September 2010 to January 2011, or the exhibition *Balenciaga and Spain* organized by Hamish Bowles and staged at the de Young Museum in San Francisco from March to July 2011.

Between 1973 and 1987, there were twelve exhibitions directly connected with the figure of Vreeland. The first, in 1973, was devoted to Balenciaga; the last was the retrospective on Yves Saint Laurent in 1983-84, the first to celebrate a living designer. The three exhibitions following the one devoted to Saint Laurent reflect the reality of a Diana Vreeland who was spending less and less time at the museum, delegating her role of special consultant to her staff (as Eleanor Dwight recalls in her biography *Diana Vreeland*. New York: HarperCollins, 2002). *Man and the Horse* was still described in the catalog as "Diana Vreeland's thirteenth exhibition" at the Met, and was to all intents and purposes a presentation of the equestrian world, one of her best-known obsessions. Like *Man and the Horse*, *The Costumes of Royal India* was one of Vreeland's exhibitions, but in both cases her staff played a fundamental part in the development and the realization of the project. Among the names we find: as exhibition coordinator Stephen Jamail (a member of her staff since 1979); as research associate Katell le Bourhis (her collaborator ever since the exhibition *The Eighteenth-Century Woman* in 1981-82); as advisors for the installation Stephen de Pietri and Simon Doonan. In Louis Rousselet's book *India of Rajahs* (Milan:

Franco Maria Ricci, 1985) published on the occasion of the exhibition *The Costumes of Royal India*, the preface is by Diana Vreeland, but the longer introduction is written by Stephen Jamail. The exhibition *Dance* again turned around one of Vreeland's favorite themes, but by this time, appearing in the catalog only as the author of a very short preface, she had taken on the guise of a "guiding spirit" for the museum (as Philippe de Montebello described her in his "Foreword"). "[Vreeland] had, after all, lived long in a world of editorial commentary. She insisted rigorously, as Stephen Jamail has testified, on the bright prospect and glorious view. Her suite of exhibitions at The Costume Institute was a glowing succession of garments in the context of bright visions, her 'big time' imagination, and the contextualization of their culture and our culture. She freed costume exhibition to participate in the new subjectivity of history and a new joy of delighted spectatorship." This is what Richard Martin and Harold Koda wrote in the catalog of the exhibition *Diana Vreeland: Immoderate Style* that they curated at the Met (December 9, 1993-March 20, 1994) to celebrate the DV style, in part through her years at the Costume Institute. Vreeland's approach to exhibiting fashion was certainly that of a fashion editor, who works by taking things away and by making novel juxtapositions that are sometimes inaccurate from a strictly historical point of view. Diana Vreeland's museum shows have suggested to curators a greater freedom in their approach to the display of fashion, thereby "involving" another protagonist: the visitor. The center of the exhibition devoted to Balenciaga was dominated by one of the historic suits of armor from the Met's Department of Arms and Armor, set astride a large white horse, since for Vreeland it was fundamental to point out the relationship that the couturier had with Spain and with a precise image of this country, not just in biographical terms, but also as a source of inspiration (and if it was not a horse, it was an elephant, like the one lent by Andy Warhol for the exhibition devoted to Hollywood on which Vreeland had placed one of Marilyn Monroe's costumes). The tour of the exhibition was accompanied by the barely hinted rhythm of flamenco; the walls were painted with the designer's favorite colors: acid green, magenta, Spanish yellow. *The 10s, The 20s, The 30s: Inventive Clothes 1909-1939*, even more elaborate and complete, is still regarded today as one of the exhibitions that had the greatest influence on American designers of the 1970s, in particular Halston. Notwithstanding the accusations of theatricality and a lack of respect for the history of costume, this was probably one of Vreeland's exhibitions most in line with that discipline, for while the large circular mirrors she utilized were flashy, they were also elements capable of giving prominence to the clothes and the aspects of their construction, revealing their complexity through reflection. Music, perfume and theatrical lighting were means of imparting a rhythm to the route through the exhibition and enveloping—and involving—the visitor. Even the choice of color as a way of emphasizing differences in theme between the rooms had become part of Vreeland's curatorial language, indeed a trademark. The checklist of the exhibition *Romantic and Glamorous Hollywood Design* was not a sequence of historical periods, or film studios, but a genuine palette that was laid out in front of our eyes: you passed from the Red Room to the Blue Room, the Emerald Green Room, the Green Room, the Beige Room and the Indigo Blue Room. The daises she designed together with the Metropolitan's technical team turned the museum into a series of stages, set at different heights, that allowed the public to walk around the clothes and Vreeland to create connections and quasi-cinematic sequences through the mannequins (and their extreme gestures) on display.

The very elements that made Diana Vreeland's exhibitions legendary are also at the bottom of the criticisms made of her work over the course of the last twenty years. Valerie Cumming, summing up a position shared by more rigorous dress historians, has written that "Diana Vreeland reinvented costume exhibitions as glossy extravaganzas, fashionable social occasions, and introduced the concept of the hagiography of living designers. After her death in 1989 [...] she had set a pattern that is still being followed: glamour, erratic scholarship and maximum celebrity appeal" (*Understanding Fashion History*. London: B.T. Batsford, 2004, p. 72). Ralph Lauren's sponsorship of the exhibition *Man and the Horse*, or the release of Saint-Laurent's perfume *Opium* into the air during the exhibition *The Manchu Dragon*, introduced the problem of commercialization into the debate over fashion exhibitions. Thinking along these lines, Lou Taylor has written: "At issue today, however, is whether the current levels of commercial sponsorship are compromising scholarly independence within exhibition research, interpretation and publication" (*Establishing Dress History*. Manchester-New York: Manchester University Press, 2004, p. 288).

But this is not the viewpoint that we have chosen to adopt in our examination of Vreeland's exhibitions. We have preferred to practice the cultural gesture of "re-viewing" in an oblique way. In this case, re-viewing Vreeland's exhibitions signifies looking at them again with oday's eyes through a series of reviews that date from the years in which those exhibitions were prepared and opened to the public. We have used articles from *Time*, *New York Magazine* and *The New Yorker*, published between 1973 and 1985. With just one exception: the catalog of the exhibition *Vanity Fair*, from 1977. Where both Philippe de Montebello, director of the Metropolitan, and Stella Blum, curator of the Costume Institute, examine (and acknowledge) Vreeland's work from the internal perspective of the museum. The museum and the special consultant: different viewpoints which meet in the exhibition that presents the collection of the Costume Institute. Not an anthology in chronological order, but a personal choice, guided by the gaze of Diana Vreeland. Who said of herself in *Allure*, in 1980: "I have astigmatism, like El Greco. I'm not comparing myself with El Greco for a minute, except that we both have the same physical disability. Partly because of his disability he saw things that most people don't see. I see all sorts of things that you don't see."

At the Met Ms. Vreeland works just as hard as she did at the magazines. She involves herself in every aspect of her shows, dealing in detail with painters, electricians, and carpenters. At first the sedate pace of the museum disturbed her. "How do you get anything done here?" she protested. "There isn't even a Telex in the place?" Everybody agrees she is a marvelous merger of luxury and practicality. Says ex-*Life* Fashion Editor Sally Kirkland: "Diana loves luxury as an art form and she admires those who use it well. But she was one of the first to promote practical American clothes, Claire McCardell, denim." And in spite of the current unluxurious state of fashion, Ms. Vreeland is not all depressed. "The success of the Balenciaga show absolutely staggered me," she said. "There's still such an interest in quality. Two hundred thousand people came to see that show. People are always interested in beauty."
"Diana Vreeland: Fashion's Empress Decrees a Delicious Occasion." *New York Magazine*, December 17, 1977, p. 95

[...] We looked at the show. It was extraordinarily well done. There were clothes from 1909 to 1939, by Poiret, Callot Soeurs, Vionnet, Chanel, and Schiaparelli, displayed on remarkable mannequins that were, variously, black, shiny white, and silver. All the mannequins were contorted in inventive ways,

and many had strange stockings pulled over their faces. The clothes had a sense of intelligent artifice, and impeccable craftsmanship, and from time to time [...], a sense of humor. [...] We talked to Diana Vreeland, the distinguished woman who put the show together. She spoke with considerable enthusiasm of the cut of a dress by Vionnet. "Cut on the bias, of course," Mrs. Vreeland said. "She knew how to do it perfectly. It hangs on the body to perfection and there isn't a single seam."
George W.S. Trow, "The Talk of the Town: Inventive." *The New Yorker*, December 24, 1973, pp. 31-2

When New York's Metropolitan Museum decided to popularize its Costume Institute, it turned to the former *Vogue* editor Diana Vreeland, a grandmother in her 70s, who is still known in the better-dressed capitals of the world as "the High Priestess of Fashion." For the museum it proved an inspired choice. Under her aegis, and with the help of a splendid staff, two years ago she produced her fashion spectacular, "The World of Balenciaga"—of which maverick designer Halston said, "Totally inspiring and at the height of elegance." Next came a show celebrating the '10s, the '20s and the '30s, ogled by thousands. Her newest show, "Romantic and Glamorous Hollywood Design," is likely to be her biggest box-office draw.
"Diana Vreeland Knows How to Pack a Museum." *People*, December 9, 1974, p. 14

"But my *dear*," said Mrs. Vreeland, her voice achieving in the small room much of the effect that Sensurround does in movie theaters, "those wrapped heads are my *greatest achievement*." [...] On the day of my visit, Mrs. Vreeland was wearing a pink shirt, a little Missoni knit vest, a calf-length black skirt, and an ivory jewel. She moved her hands with a jaunty grace. She sat behind a crowded desk, and she smoked a Lucky Strike. Her concerns on that day, she said, had to do with the condition of the costumes and the suitability of the mannequins. [...] Mrs. Vreeland professed to despair, however, over the suitability of the mannequins. "Really," she said, "I cannot *forgive* the mannequin-makers. Of course these mannequins are for selling clothes in shop windows—we understand that—but does anyone need ears that *stick out* to sell a dress? And from the hip to the knee—well, it's no glorification of the American woman, I can tell you that. It's a very short line. There's no ecstasy! What to do! What to do! Well, *first* of all we knock off all the bosoms.

All the ba-zooms go. We had a little Japanese carpenter with a tiny little saw—exquisite instrument—and he goes rat-a-tat... boom! Rat-a-tat... boom! I mean, he was doing fifteen ba-zooms a minute. Ba-zooms were falling. The guards were going absolutely dotty. And then we started to get a little bit more *line*." [...] The Costume Institute occupies a number of low-ceilinged rooms that were renovated in the late nineteen-sixties, by Edward Durell Stone, in a manner that the Costume Institute has found not completely useful. Mr. Stone's lighting system is not used; a fountain he put there has been covered up and a livelier, more theatrical effect sought after. For Mrs. Vreeland's shows, costumes are displayed more dramatically than Mr. Stone's plans allowed for. To light the costumes, Mrs. Vreeland relies on a talented man named LeMar Terry. Mr. Terry relies on light tracks. "We light the *costume*, don't you see," Mrs. Vreeland said. "Not the head." [...] On the day "Romantic and Glamorous Hollywood Design" was to open [...] I walked through the show with Mrs. Vreeland again. [...] All Mrs. Vreeland's mannequins were in place, and costumed, and all of them had stockings over their heads so they looked as though they were smothering.

A few of Mrs. Vreeland's assistants, including a tall young black man named André Leon Talley, continued to work on the mannequins—rewrapping heads, and such. [...] This caused some anxiety to Stuart Silver, who is administrator for design at the Metropolitan, and whose workmen wanted the mannequins to be finally in place, so

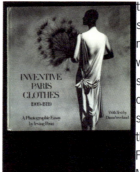

that the lighting could be finally set and the base of each mannequin painted to blend with the platform on which it stood. [...] On the night of the opening, I walked through the show with André. [...] "She is the only one I want to work for. From now on, I work only for Mrs. V. Have you seen Judy Garland? Mrs. V told me, 'André, put a trunk in front of Judy Garland and put the initials J.G. on it.' This is typical of Mrs. V. We wanted to put a topknot on Greer Garson, and she said *no*—it would be more elegant with French braids. And it *is* more elegant with French braids." [...] The message of her shows at the Metropolitan (which, it seems to me, have had more influence on the attitude of New Yorkers towards fashion than the last thirty-six issues of any fashion magazine) appears to be "It's Good! It's Better! It's Best! It's a million miles away! But it's all yours! Come and get it!"

George W.S. Trow, "Haute, Haute, Couture." *The New Yorker*, May 26, 1975, pp. 81-8

When she left *Vogue* in 1971, [...] she took over the Costume Wing of New York's Metropolitan Museum, a dusty, forgotten corner that hardly anyone visited, put on three large shows in less than three years, and set attendance records (270,000 flocked to "Romantic and Glamorous Hollywood Design" during its first two months alone).

Ingeborg Day, "Diana Vreeland: A Velvet Hand in an Iron Glove." *Ms.*, August 1975, pp. 24-30

Diana Vreeland [...] has of course organized another show for the Costume Institute of the Metropolitan Museum. It is called "American Women of Style," and the women in question are Lady Mendl; Mrs. Charles Dana Gibson; Consuelo, Duchess of Marlborough; Mrs. John W. Garrett; Gertrude Vanderbilt Whitney; Isadora Duncan; Rita de Acosta Lydig; Irene Castle; Millicent Rogers; and Josephine Baker—except that *the* woman in question is Mrs. Vreeland herself, whose taste for what she calls "audacity" the show reflects. [...] Mrs. Vreeland took us first to see the part of the exhibit devoted to Millicent Rogers, whose designs for jewelry she particularly admires. Much of the jewelry was of precious metal hammered into strong, basic patterns. There was, as well, some American Indian jewelry, and there were a few elaborate pins, which turned out to be European Orders of Merit and Honor. [...] "Where did she get the Orders?" we asked. "Bought 'em!" said Mrs.

Vreeland. "Bought 'em! Millicent had *spirit*." [...] "We have a mannequin *crouched*," Mrs. Vreeland said, "because Josephine Baker often took that pose, as though she were about to *spring*!" Mrs. Vreeland herself crouched, but she declined to spring. "And we have the costume with the bananas, as you see." [...] "I am interested, as you can tell, in those women who were born in the eighteen-seventies and eighteen-eighties and who came into the new century with energy. It takes a sense of adventure to come into a new century, perhaps. [...] I don't think those women were afraid of *anything*."

George W.S. Trow, "The Talk of the Town: Women of Style." *The New Yorker*, December 29, 1975, pp. 15-6

[...] Vreeland insists her show is not a fashion show. "This is an exhibition to project, through the beholder's imagination, a vision of ten American women." But the show is really about eleven women of style. Vreeland is the eleventh. In showing these women who were luminaries of her earlier life—she took dancing lessons from Irene Castle, Isadora used to come to her mother's house, Mrs. Lydig, Lady Mendl, and Mrs. Rogers were good friends—she has immortalized her own world. And Vreeland can certainly hold her own with these women who were creative, influential, adventurous, charitable, productive, and involved in beauty.

Joan Kron, "Exhibition-ism: History as Fashion Power." *New York Magazine*, January 12, 1976, p. 78

We paid a visit to Mrs. Vreeland one day last week as she was getting ready to *make it go.* [...] She was concerned about several issues having to do with her new show which is called "The Glory of Russian Costume," and which has been installed at the Metropolitan as part of a program of cultural exchange with the Soviet government. One of the issues that Mrs. Vreeland was concerned about was her urge to decorate various mannequins with Dynel braids in unusual colors. Some of the mannequins themselves were painted blood red. "I want to see blue Dynel braids on those girls, and *green*," Mrs. Vreeland told us. "But we have to—ummm—*consult*. The whole issue of the Dynel braids is being *analyzed* now." Mrs. Vreeland is not entirely used to the processes of consultation and analysis. Consultation and analysis have been necessary during the preparation of the Russian show, however, since the Russian clothes sent by the Soviet government have been accompanied by three

very competent Russian experts: Luiza Efimova, costume curator at the State Historical Museum, in Moscow; Tamara Korshunova, costume curator at The Hermitage, in Leningrad; and Nina Yarmolovich, costume restorer at the Kremlin Museums, in Moscow. Mrs. Vreeland said that she had the very highest respect for these three competent women but that she had found them unfamiliar with certain tools of her trade—like green and blue Dynel braids. [...] The exhibit focuses on two hundred years of Russian history—from 1700 to 1900—but moves as far back as the twelfth and eleventh centuries. The Russians wanted an ordered, chronological, academic display.

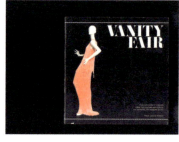

(Back in the Soviet Union, they show their costumes on the sort of headless dummies that one's grandmother had her dresses fitted on when she was somewhere else.) Mrs. Vreeland wanted magic and theatre. She got them both, in the settings, installed by Herbert Schmidt, manager of the Met's Design Department, and the designer Lucian Leone. The sophistication, the pace of work as the show was being set up, and a tape put together by Columbia Records which plays continuously in the background for "atmosphere" (if you stop listening actively for a moment to concentrate on a visual detail, you realize the "Night on Bald Mountain" has dawned into a Tchaikovsky waltz that has then moved eastward into "Scheherazade") left the Soviet women slightly breathless and confused.

George W.S. Trow and Natacha Stewart, "The Talk of the Town: Notes and Comment." *The New Yorker*, December 20, 1976, pp. 27-30

Exhibition catalogs, whatever form they may take, deal primarily with the objects on view. This publication on the Costume Institute's exhibition *Vanity Fair* has a different emphasis. It may well disappoint those looking for a digest of history of costume, chronologies, biographies, or stylistic analyses [...]. Instead the text is concerned with the organizer of the exhibition—a lively, whimsical text about Diana Vreeland and her fabled flair. Why? Because we are not presenting an anthology of the collection but a personal choice, Diana Vreeland's choice. And capricious it may be, but not random, Diana's well ordered caprice has yielded a succession of vivid images, captured in exciting vignettes, and not, definitely not, a potpourri.

Philippe de Montebello, from the catalog of the exhibition *Vanity Fair*, 1977

In 1972 Diana Vreeland joined the Costume Institute as Special Consultant for exhibitions. Her initial exhibition, *The World of Balenciaga*, introduced a brand new approach to costume exhibitions. In a spectacular setting a fashion designer for the first time was given the focus reserved in museums for great artists. Mrs. Vreeland continued her innovative point of view in subsequent exhibitions, *10's, 20's, 30's: Inventive Clothes, 1909-1939*; *Romantic and Glamorous Hollywood Design*; *American Women of*

Style; and the extraordinarily popular *The Glory of Russian Costume*, which attracted the staggering number of 830,000 visitors.

Stella Blum, "The Costume Institute / The Past Decade," from the catalog of the exhibition *Vanity Fair*, 1977

We happen to know that what most pleases Diana Vreeland, Special Consultant to the Costume Institute of the Metropolitan Museum, about her new show, "Fashions of the Hapsburg Era," is the saddlery. She has said it to us more than once. Mrs. Vreeland has a special way of looking at horses. She told us about it. It has to do with the horse itself, but only as a powerful source of simple energy. What Mrs. Vreeland likes is a source of simple energy so powerful that something rather excessive can be elaborated from what rises to the surface. In the case of horses, this is what Mrs. Vreeland calls the turnout. She talked to us about it in her office at the Metropolitan a few days before the opening of the Hapsburg show. "It's the *point*," she said. "It's important to make the point; it's important to *get* the point. The point is the *gleam*. It's what the nineteenth century knew. The gleam, the positiveness, the *turnout*." Mrs. Vreeland said that in search of the right gleam she had cabled to Vienna for permission to polish the twenty-two boots and shoes she has in the show and to polish the brass. The permission had been granted, she said, and the boots had been polished to a very high gleam and the brass polished with a soft cloth. [...] It is an opinion of Mrs. Vreeland's (and a worry to her) that the Empress Elizabeth is not as well known to the American public as she deserves to be. Mrs. Vreeland said, "People come, I talk about Elizabeth. I talk about her waist. They get that part. That is was a very thin waist. But I explain that we all did have very thin waists. [...] You get the waist you want in the end. People understand that. [...] You talk for a while and then they say, 'But who was she, this Elizabeth?' There is no history known in this country. I have been shocked." [...] Mrs. Vreeland took us through the galleries where her show was being prepared. [...] Mrs. Vreeland said she particularly liked the Hungarian uniforms. "Whenever you see the stone-marten fur and the braiding, you know you are in Hungary," she said. "Don't forget about Hungary. Never forget Hungary." Then [...] she led us to see a saddle. The label said, "Hungarian Horse Furniture, 17th Century." [...] The seat was of a pale-rose-colored velvet. The ends of the saddle, under the pommel and the cantle, were of silver set with semiprecious stones. Mrs. Vreeland said, "*There*."

George W.S. Trow, "The Talk of the Town: Turnout." *The New Yorker*, December 17, 1979, p. 38

"Forget her lack of integrity to a period; she gives visibility to the Costume Institute no money could buy," says one museum official who requested anonymity. Mrs. Vreeland herself blinks at the raised eyebrows of others: "I suppose I am difficult to work with, but I never have time to think of that. I give attention to beauty, extract facts and create a picture. And I never have unattractive thoughts. I won't allow them." *The Eighteenth-Century Woman* exhibit [...] is a show of historical lavishness gilded by Vreeland élan: she sends perfume through the ventilation systems [...]. She pipes in appropriate music

[...]. She paints mannequins in untraditional colors such as mauve, yellow, coral, red or cobalt. She decorates the walls with paintings and tapestries of the period, among them a nine-foot-high portrait of Marie Antoinette painted by her friend Elizabeth Vigée-Le Brun in 1790 and borrowed from Versailles.

André Leon Talley, "Vreeland's Show." *The New York Times*, December 6, 1981, p. 192

For all the hysteria she can create within the Costume Institute, Mrs. Vreeland has constantly been its most effective ambassador. In 1975, she travelled to Moscow with Thomas Hoving, then the director of the Met, to ask the Russian government for costumes from the Hermitage and the Kremlin. For most of the first meeting, she was uncharacteristically silent. Finally, she asked if she might say a word. "Gentlemen, in all my years of travel," she began, pausing dramatically while Hoving feared the worst, "I have *never* seen people in the streets with such... *chic*. Those *cheekbones*, the *simplicity* of the dress: I've never seen *anything* like it." It was the last thing the Russians expected to hear from Diana Vreeland. The Met got the collection—and the Russian show drew more than 800,000 visitors in its ten months at the Met. [...] She calls her office up to 100 times a day to confer with her aide-de-camp, Stephen Jamail [...]. If she goes to the museum, it is usually for a few hours and always in the afternoon. "On those days, when I take her home at night, it's the most crucial part of the day," Stephen says. "We do some of our best work in that ten-minute cab ride." This was not the kind of relationship Jamail anticipated when he was temporarily assigned to her office in 1979.

"The first week, I didn't understand a word she said," he recalls. "She'd talk about people—living and dead—as if I knew them. I was too embarrassed to say I didn't. Finally, I said, 'Mrs. Vreeland, I don't always know what you're talking about.' She said, 'Well, you're a fool for not asking.'" So he asked—and became indispensable. When Mrs. Vreeland travels now in search of costumes, Stephen Jamail is her companion.

Jesse Kornbluth, "The Empress of Clothes." *New York Magazine*, November 29, 1982, pp. 30-6

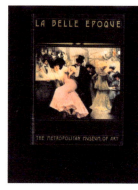

150 costumes in the Metropolitan Museum's "La Belle Époque" exhibit span the period from 1890 to 1914 and include the three shown here. During those years, fashion evolved from the controlled Victorian hourglass figure to the Art Nouveau extravagance of the Edwardian era to the more relaxed styles of the twentieth century. "La Belle Époque was a very dashing and invigorating period," says Diana Vreeland. "It was a time of great innovation—the camera, the airplane, the automobile, electricity. Life was becoming what it is today."

Anna Wintour, "La Belle Époque." With illustrations by Alexander S. Vethers. *New York Magazine*, November 29, 1982, pp. 38-41

"La Belle Époque," the new show of period high fashion organized by Diana Vreeland for New York City's Metropolitan Museum of Art and underwritten by Pierre Cardin, is an eyeful and a noseful. The eye is ravished by a theatrical assembly of more than 150 women's, men's and children's costumes, representing thousands of yards of fabric coaxed into stunning shape with a skill and diligence that today cannot be had anywhere outside of major surgery. The olfactory nerve, meantime, gets a good working over from *L'HeureBleue*, a Guerlain scent that is sprayed every morning throughout the galleries. The senses reel. They are meant to. This is not art—if clothes may be called art at all—meant to be pondered and absorbed. This is curatorial show business of a particularly shrewd order. With the humble addition of a light show and the sale of Pharmaceuticals at the ticket counter, "La Belle Époque" could be honestly promoted as a real time trip. Vreeland's ten previous collaborations with

the museum's Costume Institute have been both hot tickets and publicity bonanzas, and "La Belle Époque" shows every sign of being a smash too. The women's gowns of the era, which by Vreeland's chronology developed in the last half of the 19th century and ended on the eve of the first World War, were opulent and imperial. [...] Worth, Doucet, Callot Soeurs, Poiret: the great fashion houses are all represented with gowns and dresses that seem to challenge, in some cases even exceed, the outer limits of craftsmanship [...]. A gown by Worth was more effective than a quip that silenced a rival. Its beauty seemed inviolate: 19th century social armor. [...] There is a grandiose theatricality about the entire exhibition that, ultimately, gives the clothing a secondary role. For all the sensory overload—the perfume, rooms decorated (courtesy of Cardin) to look like Maxim's, the Offenbach piped in like a sound track for an ancient travelogue—"La Belle Époque" is less an evocation of mood or an exhibition of high style than it is an exaltation of swank, of money, of society. In that sense it is about fashion, not clothes, historical re-creation without historical perspective. [...] Nostalgia may waft through these corridors like *L'HeureBleue*, but it is based in longing not for a vanished elegance but for trammeled privilege and status cut on the bias. Remembrance of rank past.

Jay Cocks, "Living: Puttin' on the Ritz in Gotham." *Time*, January 10, 1983

The first impression is one of vitality and variety. The exhibition rooms of the Costume Institute at New York City's Metropolitan Museum of Art are bursting with lavish clothes: swift little contemporary silhouettes; magnificent ball gowns seemingly from a grander, more inert age; fantastical garments of no recognizable provenance. A few are so ugly that the eye looks away; many more are heartbreakingly lovely. They are all the work of one man: Yves Saint Laurent, 47, the most famous and influential clothing designer in the world, the king of fashion. Saint Laurent is the first person to be honored with a Metropolitan retrospective

while he is still active. (The only other couturier to have been the subject of a one-man show at the Met: the Spanish designer Cristobal Balenciaga, in 1973.) The choice was made by the museum's director and by the Costume Institute's special consultant, Diana Vreeland, whose judgment it reflects. Says the legendary former editor of *Vogue* and *Harper's Bazaar*, with the certitude and gusto that she has retained into her eighth decade: "Saint Laurent has been built into the history of fashion now for a long time. Twenty-six years is the proof that he can please most of the people most of the time four times a year. That's quite a reputation." [...] These magnificent dresses—themselves worth a visit to the show—provide the dramatic centerpiece for the exhibition that lacks logic. Vreeland's practice of organizing the Met's fashion displays by color, mood, line and occasionally whim is not satisfactory. It is impossible to trace Saint Laurent's career or to see the variety in a given year without making the crowded circuit several times and squinting down at the labels. This is particularly frustrating, since

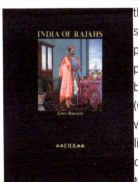

the exhibition rooms, possibly suggesting the museum's priorities, are cramped and poky. One strategy might be to go over the catalog (Clarkson N. Potter; $35), which contains chronological listings as well as a profusion of pictures.

Martha Duffy, "Living: Toasting Saint Laurent." *Time*, December 12, 1983

"Spit and polish and great tailoring" is the way Diana Vreeland describes the equestrian world. To illustrate her view, she's created "Man and the Horse," opening at the Metropolitan Museum's Costume Institute December 18. The exhibit's habits, harnesses, paintings, and carriages trace the evolution of riding clothes and accoutrements through three centuries.

Wendy Goodman, "Man & the Horse: Diana Vreeland's Latest Costume

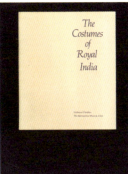

Extravaganza." *New York Magazine*, November 26, 1984, pp. 65-72

So "Costumes of Royal India," of which this fabulous piece of cotton is just a small part, springs into New York City's Metropolitan Museum of Art with a vitality and dignity well beyond that of most exhibitions of clothing. All is ravishment: a child's coat made of silver fabric embroidered with gold thread; a woman's costume of veil, tunic and pajamas that plays with sunset shades of gold and violet. Fashion and society are the prevailing standards that squeeze museum costume shows tight, but "Costumes of Royal India" celebrates an ongoing tradition—of craft, of coloration, of symbolic dress and functional wear. Diana Vreeland, who in her years as a fashion doyen coined a neat line about Indian dress ("Pink is the navy blue of India"), started to organize this show more than a year and a half ago, and her trademarks are abundant. There are atmospheric tapes of Indian court music, elaborate furniture, and the scent of a specially made Guerlain sandalwood to orchestrate the clothes. This kind of show-biz gilding draws the crowds, but the hues and density and drapings of the clothes, the impact of their easy and erotic majesty, will linger much longer than the perfume.

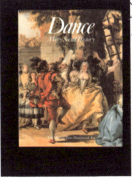

Jay Cocks and Elizabeth Rudulph, "Living: A Harmony of Fugitive Color." *Time*, December 16, 1985

DIANA VREELAND

"Diana Vreeland: Immoderate Style" opens on December 9th at the Costume Institute of the Metropolitan Museum of Art.

210

DV: An Edited Chronology

In the summer of 1903, Diana Dalziel was born in Paris, on the cusp of a century she would come to experience and influence by way of fashion.

Diana attributed her "extraordinary visual sense" to having been born in Paris, where she spent periods of her formative years, even after her parents emigrated to New York City in 1904.

Diana's mother, Emily Key Hoffman, was an American socialite of great beauty and charisma, who moved in both aristocratic and bohemian circles of the Belle Époque on both sides of the Atlantic. Her father, Frederick Dalziel, was of Scottish descent, but had grown up in London, where he married Emily two years prior to Diana's birth.

By virtue of her parents' friendships and social circles, young Diana was exposed to personalities, locales and events that would impact greatly upon her aesthetic sensibilities. As a child, Diana attended the coronation of George V, was a flower girl at the wedding of Gloria Gould to Lord Decies, and met Diaghilev and Nijinsky, who were guests at her mother's home. By the time World War I made transatlantic travel impossible, Diana had already visited the great capitals of Europe and had known their splendor, rituals and personalities.

Diana herself, although enmeshed in a world of beauty and elegance, was displeased by her own physical appearance, especially in comparison to her younger sister, Alexandra who was born in 1907. Diana's adolescent diary chronicles her quest for self-improvement via hard work, cultivation of manners and knowledge, and the creative determinism to invent herself in her own image of the ideal woman—charming, distinctive and elegant.

In 1922, her coming out was celebrated at the Ritz-Carlton in New York City, with Diana wearing a white satin-fringed dress based on a model by Poiret, red velvet slippers and a corsage of camellias. Years later, when "discovered" by editor of *Harper's Bazaar*, Carmel Snow, Diana was also attired in white with red accents, a visual theme which would appear frequently in her future editorial work.

In 1923, Diana met Reed Vreeland, a Yale graduate from upstate New York, whom she married the following year. Shortly after marrying the couple moved to Albany, where Diana settled happily into married life. She gave birth to two sons Thomas in 1925, and Frederick in 1927, before the Vreelands moved to London when Reed took a position in the Foreign Department of the Guaranty Trust Company.

During their time in London, residing at Hanover Terrace, near Regent's Park, Diana and Reed moved in the circles of European social and cultural elite. Diana frequented French couture houses, and cultivated friendships with luminaries such as Evelyn Waugh, Gabrielle Chanel, Elsa Maxwell, Noel Coward, Cecil Beaton and Christian Berard. Near the end of the Vreelands' six-year sojourn in England, Diana was one of fifteen American women presented at Court to King George V and Queen Mary in May of 1933.

Despite their comfortable economic position, and Diana's recent inheritance from her mother, she recalled London as terribly expensive, and opened a lingerie shop on Berkeley Square to supplement the family income. As proprietress of a luxury shop, Diana further cultivated her taste for elegant clothes and textiles, and inevitably honed her sense for suggesting ways in which women could infuse their lives with glamour through clothing.

After returning to America, the stylish sophistication and fashion confidence Diana garnered during her years abroad earned the notice of *Harper's Bazaar* editor Carmel Snow, who offered her a job as the magazine's fashion editor after spotting her dancing at the St. Regis Hotel wearing a white lace Chanel dress, with a bolero and red roses in her hair. Thus, in 1936, with her only prior work experience having been running her small shop, Diana embarked upon a four decade long career as a magazine editor, fashion journalist and consummate tastemaker.

Her first gesture at *Harpers's Bazaar* was to scribe the fashion and lifestyle advice column, "Why Don't You?" which rapidly garnered popularity and notoriety for its quirky combination of fantastical and practical advice for women. "Why Don't You?" suggested creative self invention above all, whether it be by recommending wearing unlikely ensembles such as "wool jersey pyjamas and a short-sleeved pull-over of solid black paillettes, no jewelry and Norwegian moccasin slippers copied in black satin piped in gold," or with more utilitarian but no less inventive prescriptions such as "Why don't you find some Victorian cufflinks and have them made into studs for the front of a pleated silk blouse?"

By 1939, Diana Vreeland was full time fashion editor of *Harpers's Bazaar*. She forged fruitful working relationships with prominent fashion designers, photographers and models, alchemising these friendships into creative collaborations that steered the fashion aesthetic of the age.

During the war years, *Harpers's Bazaar* was instrumental in promoting American fashions and encouraging fortitude on the home front. As Paris fashions disappeared from the pages of *Harpers's Bazaar*, Vreeland engineered images that celebrated American design and sensibilities, such as Louise Dahl-Wolfe's iconic location shoot that set Claire McCardell's easy sportswear against the backdrop of dramatic American landscapes and architecture including a Frank Lloyd Wright house near Tucson, Arizona.

After the war, *Harpers's Bazaar* under Vreeland introduced Dior's New Look, the bikini, and new faces in entertainment and fashion, as well as new ideals of beauty and grace with models such as Dovima, Suzy Parker and Dorian Leigh.

By 1957, Diana had become a fashion figure formidable enough to inspire lampoon on the silver screen. *Funny Face* parodied Vreeland in the character of tyrannical but pithy fashion editor and brought the rarefied world of fashion magazines down to earth with humor. Although being the subject of satire displeased Diana highly, the film marks the moment when, as noted by her biographer Eleanor Dwight, the "Vreeland-inspired character of the fashion editor became an American icon."

Diana later said that no one in the world had a better spot in a better time than she had in the 1960s. She embraced the new decade wholly, ensuring that the new fashions, personalities, and optimism were evident in her work. For Diana, as for the world, it was time for a change, and in 1962, after nearly 26 years at *Harpers's Bazaar*, the *New York Times* heralded her fashion defection from *Harper's Bazaar* with the headline: "Diana Vreeland Dynamic Fashion Figure Joins *Vogue*."

The new position at *Vogue* afforded Diana the opportunity and creative freedom to take the magazine and its readers to new heights of fashion fantasy; exotic locations, luminous personalities, exciting designs and ever more innovative fashion styling. The new and eclectic beauty ideals that came to be celebrated in the decade had already been long-championed by Vreeland. Her admiration for the youthquake generation, and British culture put legends of 1960s "swinging London," such as Mick Jagger, Mary Quant, the Beatles and Twiggy into the American spotlight.

After Reed Vreeland's death, for which she mourned deeply but privately, Diana even more fully embraced her role as youthful veteran of style, and conduit of the new, via her professional and social life.

JENNA ROSSI-CAMUS

However, by the late 1960s, Vreeland's extravagance was proving unmanageable for *Vogue* financially, and a new practicality in fashion was edging out the hyperbolic fantasy of her aesthetic. In 1971, aged 68, she was relieved of editorship of *Vogue*, and the role was passed on to her longtime assistant Grace Mirabella.

Shortly thereafter, in 1972, she was invited by Thomas Hoving, director of the Metropolitan Museum of Art, to serve the Costume Institute as special consultant. In this new role Vreeland was to generate ideas for exhibitions and their design and to suggest materials and sources for addition to the Costume Institute's holdings.
At the museum, during her seventeen year tenure, via fifteen exhibitions, she translated her editorial language into a curatorial one and empowered museum visitors to experience fashion as an immersive sensory experience.

In 1977, Diana was subject of the fabled *Rolling Stone* interview and shared colorful reflections on her life, career and memories of the 20th century with reporter Lally Weymouth. At the time, Diana was fully entrenched in the world of the museum, and shines as a great storyteller whose perennially quotable assertions are possessed of wit, intelligence and a touch of absurdity.

In 1980, Vreeland published *Allure*, a compendium of black and white photography from her earlier work and archives, annotated and captioned by her anecdotes, remembrances and suggestions. *Allure* was a foray back into print for Diana, and was followed shortly after by the publishing of her autobiography *D.V.*, in 1984. In the memoir, she recounts her life story, as a series of both undeniable and improbable experiences, and shares her philosophy on almost everything.

On August 2, 1989, Diana Vreeland passed away at her home in New York City. At her memorial service, held at the Metropolitan Museum of Art, Richard Avedon delivered her often quoted eulogy, in which he succinctly declared that Diana, "lived for imagination ruled by discipline and created a totally new profession. Vreeland invented the fashion editor."

In 1993, the museum further honored her with the exhibition *Diana Vreeland: Immoderate Style*, which celebrated her life, career, personality and impact upon the Costume Institute and successive exhibitions of fashion. Since then, Diana has been the subject of numerous publications, exhibitions, films and the off-Broadway play *Full Gallop*. Her editorial work perennially inspires photographers, stylists, editors and designers, and in 2009, *Harper's Bazaar* dedicated a shoot entirely to recreating iconic photos of Diana, with Sarah Jessica Parker standing in as Vreeland herself.

In 2011, Diana's granddaughter-in-law, Lisa Immordino Vreeland, produced a documentary film and book dedicated to her work and legacy entitled *The Eye Has To Travel*.

There is no danger of Diana Vreeland's spirit fading from memory, and indeed her influence seems to grow ever stronger the more we examine her life and work. She professed to "loathe nostalgia," and thus when reflecting upon her contributions, she seems to encourage us not to look back but ahead—reminding us as that, "fashion is on the daily air, it keeps coming," and to keep looking, as she did every moment of her life, for the "suggestion of something we've never seen."

Some "Why Don't You...?"

Her first appearance in *Harper's Bazaar*, in March 1936, was as the writer of the column "Why Don't You...?": "Why don't you... zip yourself into your evening dresses? Waft a big bouquet about like a fairy wand? Wear a bowler? Stick Japanese hair-pins in your hair? Buy a transparent evening coat? Or a geranium chiffon toque? Or bright flannel gloves? Or a black blouse? Expose your fortune in an isinglass bag? Hide your hips under an accordion-pleated jacket? Wear fruit hats? Currants? Cherries?"

Made up by that wizard of graphics Alexey Brodovitch, the column was an immediate sensation. It was extreme, highly imaginative, utterly snobbish. In her memoirs, she limited herself to saying that: "It was rather frivolous. I don't remember too many of the ideas, thank *goodness*." What came across in the articles was her taste for the extraordinary and her great intuition: fashion feeds on dreams and absurdities. Even the intellectual *The New Yorker* took notice and wrote about her, parodying the column.

"For a coat to put on after skiing, get yourself an Italian driver's, of red-orange lined in dark green." That was one of her ideas. Or: "Have a furry elk-kid trunk for the back of your car." In her memoirs she said: "They were all very tried and true ideas, mind you. We had a trunk like that on the back of our Bugatti. 'Knit yourself a little skullcap. Turn your ermine coat into a bathrobe.'" But among the ones that attracted most attention was: "Why don't you... rinse your blond child's hair in dead champagne to keep its gold, as they do in France?"
MLF

WHY DON'T YOU . . .

ZIP YOURSELF INTO YOUR EVENING DRESSES?

WAFT A BIG BOUQUET ABOUT LIKE A FAIRY WAND?

WEAR A BOWLER?

STICK JAPANESE HAIR-PINS IN YOUR HAIR?

BUY A TRANSPARENT EVENING COAT?

OR A GERANIUM CHIFFON TOQUE?

OR BRIGHT FLANNEL GLOVES?

OR A BLACK BLOUSE?

EXPOSE YOUR FORTUNE IN AN ISINGLASS BAG?

HIDE YOUR HIPS UNDER AN ACCORDION-PLEATED JACKET?

WEAR FRUIT HATS?

CURRANTS?

CHERRIES?

JEAN MORAL

Or lift your blue wool Mainbocher skirt to show a candy-striped petticoat? (Bloomingdale)

Why don't you, some hot day, collect your child's curls in a loose hair net?

Photograph her sitting against the mirror? The full reflection is adorable.

Or pull her curls all up on top and stick garden flowers in the little black velvet bow?

Why don't you put your little girl in white swiss dotted in pink with pink satin bows on the shoulder?

— and a matching dotted-swiss coat with a big cape collar and a pink satin lining?

Put a schoolgirl in culottes and a jacket of gray or navy flannel, herringbone or dark green tweed?

Make a yellow flannel dressing-gown with a little hood in back?

why don't
by

216

If you can do point de Turque,
why don't you make your baby
a top sheet and pillow-slip
encrusted with myriad
stars of all sizes?

you

and Vreeland

Cut your little girl's
hair with a bang
and tie it with a
black velvet ribbon?

Why don't you design monograms with
circles around them for the pockets of your
children's cardigans and the
sleeves of their dressing-gowns?

Keep the hair out of her eyes
like this, with one long
braid tied with a
brown velvet ribbon?

you put them in cherry
velvet pyjamas for supper
bath and then change
bedtime into sleeping pyjamas?

Why don't you, on a very dark sunburned
child with thick hair like a tassel, put
a dirndl dress of white shantung with no
sleeves, no socks and bright yellow kid sandals?

Jeana.

91

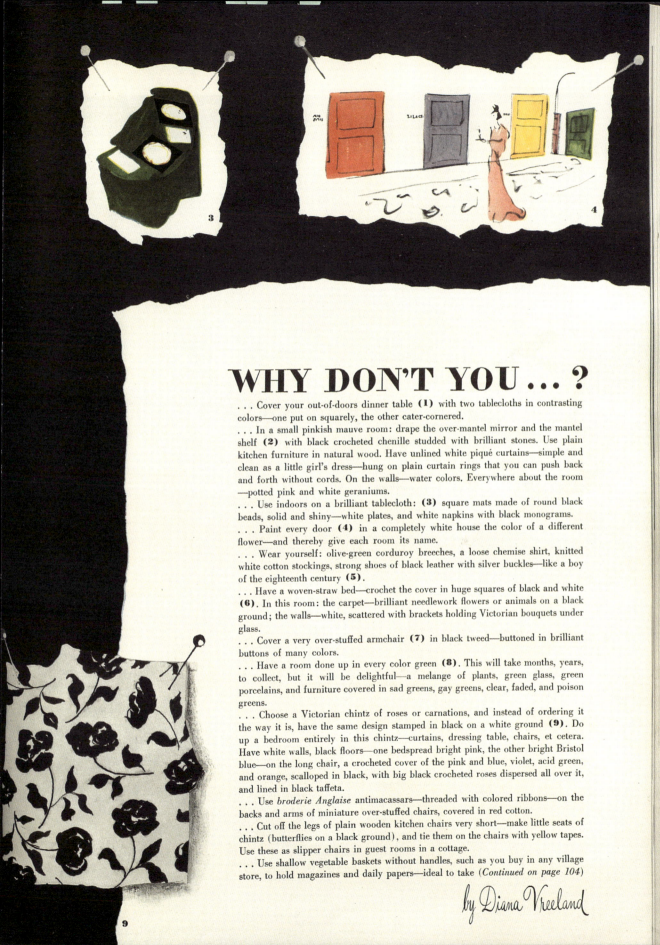

WHY DON'T YOU...?

. . . Cover your out-of-doors dinner table **(1)** with two tablecloths in contrasting colors—one put on squarely, the other cater-cornered.

. . . In a small pinkish mauve room: drape the over-mantel mirror and the mantel shelf **(2)** with black crocheted chenille studded with brilliant stones. Use plain kitchen furniture in natural wood. Have unlined white piqué curtains—simple and clean as a little girl's dress—hung on plain curtain rings that you can push back and forth without cords. On the walls—water colors. Everywhere about the room —potted pink and white geraniums.

. . . Use indoors on a brilliant tablecloth: **(3)** square mats made of round black beads, solid and shiny—white plates, and white napkins with black monograms.

. . . Paint every door **(4)** in a completely white house the color of a different flower—and thereby give each room its name.

. . . Wear yourself: olive-green corduroy breeches, a loose chemise shirt, knitted white cotton stockings, strong shoes of black leather with silver buckles—like a boy of the eighteenth century **(5)**.

. . . Have a woven-straw bed—crochet the cover in huge squares of black and white **(6)**. In this room: the carpet—brilliant needlework flowers or animals on a black ground; the walls—white, scattered with brackets holding Victorian bouquets under glass.

. . . Cover a very over-stuffed armchair **(7)** in black tweed—buttoned in brilliant buttons of many colors.

. . . Have a room done up in every color green **(8)**. This will take months, years, to collect, but it will be delightful—a melange of plants, green glass, green porcelains, and furniture covered in sad greens, gay greens, clear, faded, and poison greens.

. . . Choose a Victorian chintz of roses or carnations, and instead of ordering it the way it is, have the same design stamped in black on a white ground **(9)**. Do up a bedroom entirely in this chintz—curtains, dressing table, chairs, et cetera. Have white walls, black floors—one bedspread bright pink, the other bright Bristol blue—on the long chair, a crocheted cover of the pink and blue, violet, acid green, and orange, scalloped in black, with big black crocheted roses dispersed all over it, and lined in black taffeta.

. . . Use *broderie Anglaise* antimacassars—threaded with colored ribbons—on the backs and arms of miniature over-stuffed chairs, covered in red cotton.

. . . Cut off the legs of plain wooden kitchen chairs very short—make little seats of chintz (butterflies on a black ground), and tie them on the chairs with yellow tapes. Use these as slipper chairs in guest rooms in a cottage.

. . . Use shallow vegetable baskets without handles, such as you buy in any village store, to hold magazines and daily papers—ideal to take (Continued on page 104)

by Diana Vreeland

by DIANA VREELAND

—tie an enormous bunch of silver balloons on the foot of your child's bed on Christmas Eve?

—give someone an enormous white handkerchief-linen table-cloth, and in different handwriting and in different colors (black, acid green, pink, scarlet and pale blue) have embroidered all the bons mots you can possibly think of?

—give a case of *vin rosé*—a delicious wine for luncheon or for simple dinners? (This can be had from Labourdette.)

—go to Dazians, the theatrical material shop, and buy some of their dazzling Cellophane material or artificial gold or silver cloth to do up your Christmas table?

—give white handkerchief-linen sheets and pillows? Very, very fine linen, inlaid with wide Valenciennes, such as your mother used in her trousseau, with big eyelets for pale pink satin ribbon, threaded through and tied in bows. Your most luxurious friend won't have these and she will adore them in contrast with her more modern ones of satin or crepe de chine.

Why don't you give a length of exquisite brocade—enough for an evening envelope, to bind a favorite book, or make a little jacket.

—give to the wife of your favorite band leader an entire jazz-band made of tiny baguette diamonds and cabochon emeralds, in the form of a bracelet from Marcus?

—give one of the most alluring things we've seen—an enormous round Cellophane bandbox, tied with beautiful ribbons and stuffed with colored papers and all manner of beautifying creams and lotions from Elizabeth Arden?

—give your greatest friend a Lanz jacket of bright red Wamsutta ski cloth with silver buttons? This would be equally smart with shorts in the South, with ski pants, over a black dress indoors on a chilly day, or sitting up in bed.

Why don't you ask for a Skye terrier?

—ask for thin pink linen sheets with big pink linen ruffles? Meticulously ironed—the effect is fresh and delicious.

—go to the Japan Paper Company before you decide on your wrappings? The variety of such excellent taste is amazing.

—give a beautiful beaded belt to wear with fur tunics? Jaeckel has them.

—remember some of the lovely head-dresses Antoine is showing —iridescent roses for brunettes, a (Continued on page 122)

Vogue's Diana Vreeland

she sets the fashion

"One millimeter more? One millimeter less, hmm? That's all it takes, and the proportion would be lost," says Mrs. Vreeland, demonstrating the perfection of detail that goes into fashion by gauging a pearl. *"Jewels? I love them—but not for myself. I prefer fantaisie."* She wears white-cotton *"drugstore"* gloves *"to keep the print from getting in my nails."*

THIS STRONG-FEATURED, delicately boned woman with a funny-wry smi and polished brown-black hair has more influence on what the America woman wears today than any other single person in the fashion busines A strong statement? As editor-in-chief of *Vogue,* our leading fashic magazine (its close on-the-heels rival is *Harper's Bazaar*), she is prim *provocateur* of the new style trends. Why are we running around wit dresses above our knees? Because sixty-ish Mrs. T. Reed Vreeland Park Avenue, Southampton and Condé Nast pushed Courrèges—three years ago. She's way past that, and watch it. "All I think about now Dynel hair, marvelous stuff, made by Union Carbide." She talks ellipses, walks with an elegant lope, operates on intuition. She wa born in Paris, brought up in Europe, never went to college, nor has sh any guilt about pursuing a life of sensuous and intellectual enjoymen

PRODUCED BY PATRICIA COFFIN   PHOTOGRAPHED BY JAMES H. KARALE

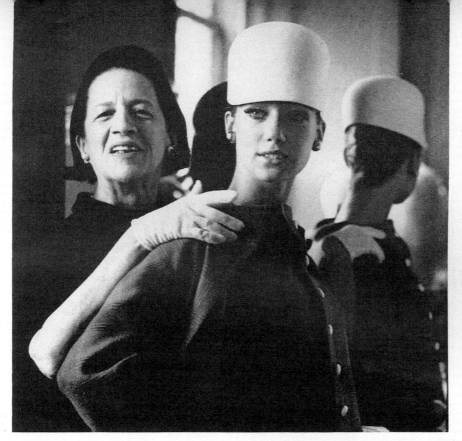

"The final run-through is IT.
We've eliminated 60 costumes
. . . chose this Monte-Sano
ensemble, Mr. John's white felt
for January. . . ." Marisa Berenson
models it in the current Vogue.
"The editors bring all their
selections from the market to me,
down to the last bracelet."

"One works best in one's own
ambience," she says,
using a Vogueism. This includes
her portrait by René Bouché
(left), a wall papered with pictures:
Callas, astronauts, Nureyev,
Hepburn, print of Agnès Sorel
portrait—one breast bared. "I use
these photos to explain things
like bias cut. . . ."

continued

"We pictured this Dynel hair in Jordan."

"I'm very nearsighted, but one can see everything one wants to . . . hmm?"

"I choose each photo, read every w
goes into the magazine," says Vre

DIANA VREELAND continued

With French Vogue's Mme. de Langlade, she calls on manufacturer Ben Zuckerman. "I feel real camaraderie for my 7th Ave. friends."

She is an exaggeration of herself

"Why have meetings? Why sit down?" asks Mrs. Vreeland, who does a vast amount of business by phone. (She has four vari-colored ones instead of extensions.) She operates 12 of the 24 hours out of a large, square, richly red room carpeted in pseudo-leopard, smelling of Rigaud's cypress-scented candles. On her black-lacquer desk: anemones ("I *adore* anemones."), masses of pads on which she jots her famous *mots justes*, layouts, folios full of manuscripts to be taken home. Meanwhile, tides of clothes, lingerie, jewels, shoes, bags daily flow in and out of her office.

What is fashion

BY DIANA VREELAND

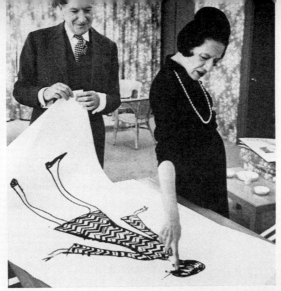

"Sassoon hair is sweeping the world," says Diana sweepingly to British designer-photographer Cecil Beaton, whose work she often uses in Vogue. Beaton wears tasseled cap for a laugh, Diana is in her classic sweater and skirt.

checks *Irving Penn* swimsuit photos. The chairs were a present from Courrèges.

"Truman can write! Cecil can photograph!" she says, emphasizing the great nonfashion talent. *"I continuously woo and seduce."* Above, she checks proofs with Truman Capote.

A NEW FASHION always appears monstrous. Like new architecture, it shocks, it breaks the rules. It is change, it gives a little air. Politicians get away with change, why not the rest of us? Fashion (a way of dressing, behaving, writing *favored at the time,* says the dictionary) is part of life, of history. It is woven into the intellectual, economic, global fabric of today as water braids itself into a single stream. Today's standards of living are so high for so many, that fashion has become part of the way of the world. The prejudiced ones, the reactionaries, cling to the old; they are guilty of nothing except missing the fun. Fashion is the reaction to the economic and social scene—everything from Cape Kennedy to the frug and the jerk. It *fits* the times. Suddenly, everyone said, "A-OK," and wore Courrèges boots, but by then, the pace setters, the daring, had moved on—with the step getting faster and faster, made possible by that great Americanism called "availability." There are no more straws in the wind; it's a stick, and it's here—supersonic, catatonic! Fashion sifts down from the top, floods, I should say, and quite as often splashes *up* (pea jackets, jeans, fishermen's sweaters). Fashion is for pruning to a woman's own form *and* circumstances. She should *use* it, not fight it, study it, observe it and then apply it, with discrimination, to herself, listen to the drum that beats for that and the lute that plays for this.

She should hail the hero of the hour, the sport of the day, the place, the fun of fashion in all of its flavors—without prejudice, with humor and understanding. Fashion is made up of opportunity and change, and is therefore for the young, of every age.

DIANA VREELAND:
A VELVET HAND IN AN IRON GLOVE

INGEBORG DAY

"You know, don't you, that the bikini is only the most important invention since the atom bomb?"

"My entire life has been the pursuit of pleasure."

"I can't imagine what it is that women supposedly don't have—unless, of course, it's money. But even then—I'd much rather have my money coming from some man, wouldn't you?"

"There is absolutely nothing extraordinary about me. I've worked for forty years, that's all."

—*Diana Vreeland*

In her mid-thirties, with a wealthy husband, two sons, and no formal education, Diana Vreeland went to work. She could claim only one marketable skill: from two decades of talking to and buying from couturiers, she knew clothes. Over the next 35 years at the two rag-trade bibles, *Harper's Bazaar* and *Vogue,* Diana Vreeland became this century's single most powerful influence on American fashion.

When she left *Vogue* in 1971, an old friend mused: "Diana will gently ease into the world of the Windsors and the other gilded retirees in their set." Instead, she took over the Costume Wing of New York's Metropolitan Museum, a dusty, forgotten corner that hardly anyone visited, put on three large shows* in less than three years, and set attendance records (270,000 flocked to "Romantic and Glamorous Hollywood Design" during its first two months alone).

"That woman is one hell of a great

---

* "The World of Balenciaga"(March 23 to June 30, 1973) ; "The Tens, the Twenties, the Thirties" (December 13, 1973 to September 3, 1974) ; "Romantic and Glamorous Hollywood Design" (November 21, 1974 to April 27, 1975).

old broad," says one ardent admirer. Other descriptions abound: a Chinese Mary Poppins, a camel, a crane with the face of a cigar-store Indian, a monster, a genius. Coco Chanel (about whom Vreeland raved in true Vreelandese: "the golden skin, the Dubonnet cheeks, the expression of a baby bull dressed like a Prussian sailor") called Vreeland "the most pretentious woman I've ever met." Designers whom she disliked denounce her as supercilious and unscrupulous. Those whom she helped to success echo Yves St. Laurent in praising her "incredible sensitivity to quality. . . ."

Born about 75 years ago in Paris, of an American mother and an English father, Diana Dalziel accompanied her parents and sister on ritual "in season" travels to Venice, Deauville, London, and Edinburgh. Schooling was scant. "We were brought up with great kindness and humor, but we were always being put into school in December and taken out April first." At the beginning of World War I, the Dalziels moved to the United States, and in 1924, Diana married T. Reed Vreeland, a young, mild-mannered American banker. They lived briefly in Albany until Reed Vreeland's business took them to Europe.

Back in New York in 1936, Diana Vreeland began to work at *Harper's Bazaar,* writing an advice column which mixed fashion and snob appeal—exactly what her readers wanted. "Why Don't You . . ." ran for years and was quoted and parodied more often than any other fashion column.

Why don't you . . .
Sweep into the drawing room on your first big night with an enormous red-fox muff of many skins?

Remember how delicious champagne cocktails are after tennis or golf? Indifferent champagne can be used for these.

Wear bare knees and long white knitted socks, as Unity Mitford does when she takes tea with Hitler at the Carlton in Munich?

Rinse your blond child's hair in dead champagne to keep its gold, as they do in France?

S. J. Perelman, who supposedly dined out for years on jokes about Vreeland pronouncements, replied to that last one, ". . . because I prefer to let my child go to hell in her own way, as they do in America."

Over the next dozen or so years as *Bazaar's* Fashion Editor, Vreeland worked long hours building a reputation and an image. One important element of her gathering fame was her, well, decisiveness. Confronted with any new fashion item, she would instantly boom either, "It's *utterly* bad," or "It's *completely* divine." By the 1950s, her appearance at a fashion show had become the highest praise a designer could hope for and proof that she or he had "arrived"—or would, soon. In 1959, she was able to summon underlings into her lacquered office, stare dramatically into space, and announce: "I see *green.*" The following year—*poof!*—clothes were green.

Her image became one of her most successful assets. Far surpassing a fashion editor's role of reporting fashion, Vreeland predicted it, set it, personified it. Outrageous and eccentric in personal appearance, speech, and opinions, she became news by creating an image so bizarre that it was instantly recognizable. She was "seen" wherever she went, listened to whenever she spoke, and quoted

Fashion/Joan Kron

EXHIBITION-ISM: HISTORY AS FASHION POWER

"...The museum not only controls fashion immortality, it has become the launching pad for new styles inspired by the past..."

Yes, there is life after death for couturiers and style-setters—if they've lived right. Museum costume exhibitions are becoming escalators to fashion heaven. And guarding the big cloakroom in the sky—the Costume Institute of the Metropolitan Museum of Art—is its highly influential special consultant, Diana Vreeland, a former editor of *Harper's Bazaar* and *Vogue*. When the imperious, red-lipped, red-finger-tipped septuagenarian departs to meet her maker, she will no doubt take with her a set of Vuitton luggage, her manicurist, and enough of her favorite red paint to recolor the Pearly Gates.

The museum's new fashion power doesn't end with its control of immortality. Its costume shows are involved with resurrection as well. Edging out the fashion magazine, the Paris runway, and the discotheque, it has become the launching pad for new style trends inspired by exhibits of bygone body wear.

Since 1972, when Vreeland joined the Met after a forced retirement from *Vogue*, her first three shows ("The World of Balenciaga," "The Tens, Twenties, and Thirties," and "Romantic and Glamorous Hollywood Design") all focused on nostalgia (which could almost qualify as one of fashion's shifting erogenous zones). And why not? Vreeland is, after all, a veteran of half a century of décolletage diplomacy. And what comes naturally to her has become the public passion. Her latest offering, "American Women of Style" (funded by a grant from SCM Corporation), which opened last month and will run through August, is packing them in. Officially, it's a Bicentennial bow to originality and rugged individualism, but it's also an ode to the good old days.

Vreeland pulled ten women (all dynamos and all dead) out of her address book (she had personally known all but two of them), and their portraits, memorabilia, and clothes (or reasonable facsimiles) out of various trunks. When she put them all together at the Met, you'd think she was selling cashmere sweaters at half price. Ten thousand people trooped through the show in the first two days. Suddenly everyone is talking about Lady Mendl's

beaded cape which Schiaparelli designed after seeing the Neptune fountain at Versailles; and about Irene Castle inventing the headache band; Isadora Duncan and Josephine Baker dancing almost nude; and Mrs. John W. Garrett's harem pants by Léon Bakst; and Millicent Rogers, who was a pioneer in wearing ethnic clothes; and Rita de Acosta Lydig, a lace freak,

who had sixteenth-century lace trim on her handmade Renaissance velvet pumps. Now it won't be long before it's all played back to us *outside* the museum. "We've been watching the rise of lace, and after this show," says Brooklyn Museum costume curator Elizabeth Ann Coleman, "it will be very big."

Just as Vreeland-the-editor influenced

Powerhouse: *Diana Vreeland sits at Isadora Duncan's feet in the Met's new show.*

Photographed by Harry Benson

Sources for Images and Quotations

5 From Diana Vreeland's introduction to the catalog of the exhibition *Man and the Horse* (New York, The Costume Institute at The Metropolitan Museum of Art, December 18, 1984-September 1, 1985)

5 Three pictures of Diana Vreeland, Andy Warhol and Fred Hughes in St. Mark's Square, Venice, summer 1973. From Eleanor Dwight, *Diana Vreeland*. New York: HarperCollins, 2002. Diana Vreeland, Andy Warhol and Fred Hughes were in Venice for the annual ball held by Countess Nathalie Volpi on the occasion of the Film Festival. © Sam Green, © HarperCollins

15 Diana Vreeland in the introduction to the book *Allure*. New York: Doubleday, 1980, p. 11
Sherrie Levine, *Statement*, 1982, now in David Evans (ed.), *Appropriation*. London-Cambridge MA, Whitechapel-The MIT Press, 2009, p. 81

22 *D.V.* Edited by George Plimpton and Christopher Hemphill. New York: Alfred A. Knopf, 1984, p. 103
D.V. Edited by George Plimpton and Christopher Hemphill. New York: Alfred A. Knopf, 1984, p. 111

23 The model Dovima in a Balenciaga domino. Ektachrome Richard Avedon. *Harper's Bazaar*, December 1950. © The Richard Avedon Foundation, © Hearst Corporation

24 Kodachrome Louise Dahl-Wolfe. *Harper's Bazaar*, February 1950. © Louise Dahl-Wolfe, © Hearst Corporation

25 A corner of the "garden in hell," Diana Vreeland's New York apartment, which she furnished with the help of her designer friend Billy Baldwin. Photo Richard Champion. Page from the book edited by Paige Rense, *Celebrity Homes: Architectural Digest Presents the Private Worlds of Thirty International Personalities*. New York: The Viking Press, 1977. © Richard Champion, © The Viking Press

26-27 Double page from the leading article "Paris: the news as we see it - a special Vogue report on the new French clothes" signed DV, with Veruschka wearing the Mondrians by Yves Saint Laurent. Photo Irving Penn. *Vogue*, September 1, 1965. © The Irving Penn Foundation, © Condé Nast

28 Page dedicated to beauty. Kodachrome George Hoyningen-Huene. Art direction Alexey Brodovitch. *Harper's Bazaar*, October 1942. © George Hoyningen-Huene, © Hearst Corporation

29 Kodachrome Karen Radkai. *Harper's Bazaar*, March 1, 1950. © Karen Radkai, © Hearst Corporation

30 Costume by Adrian for Joan Crawford in *The Bride Wore Red* (directed by Dorothy Arzner, 1937). Photo by Keith Trumbo for the book by Dale McConathy with Diana Vreeland, *Hollywood Costume. Glamour! Glitter! Romance!* (New York: Harry N. Abrams, 1976), published after the exhibition *Romantic and Glamorous Hollywood Design* curated by Diana Vreeland (New York, The Costume Institute at The Metropolitan Museum of Art, November 21, 1974-August 31, 1975). © Keith Trumbo, © Harry N. Abrams

31 Tribute to Diana Vreeland by Gianni Versace, 1990. Taken from *Diana Vreeland: Immoderate Style*, catalog for the exhibition curated by Richard Martin and Harold Koda (New York, The Costume Institute at The Metropolitan Museum of Art, December 9, 1993-March 20, 1994). New York: The Metropolitan Museum of Art, 1993. © Gianni Versace, © The Metropolitan Museum of Art

32 Introduction to Dale McConathy with Diana Vreeland, *Hollywood Costume. Glamour! Glitter! Romance!* (New York: Harry N. Abrams, 1976), published after the exhibition *Romantic and Glamorous Hollywood Design* curated by Diana Vreeland (New York, The Costume Institute at The Metropolitan Museum of Art, November 21, 1974-August 31, 1975)
D.V. Edited by George Plimpton and Christopher Hemphill. New York: Alfred A. Knopf, 1984, pp. 13-4

33 Costume by Adrian for Kay Johnson in *Madame Satan* (directed by Cecil B. DeMille, 1930). Photo by Keith Trumbo for the book by Dale McConathy with Diana Vreeland, *Hollywood Costume. Glamour! Glitter! Romance!* (New York:

Harry N. Abrams, 1976), published after the exhibition *Romantic and Glamorous Hollywood Design* curated by Diana Vreeland (New York, The Costume Institute at The Metropolitan Museum of Art, November 21, 1974-August 31, 1975). © Keith Trumbo, © Harry N. Abrams

34 "The Nine-Minute Wonder Exercises." Photo Ben Rose. *Harper's Bazaar*, April 1950. © Ben Rose, © Hearst Corporation

35 "A photograph in motion [...] of marvelous Dior's chiffon." Kodachrome Richard Avedon. *Harper's Bazaar*, December 1948. © The Richard Avedon Foundation, © Hearst Corporation

36 The flamenco of Carmen Amaya in a cafe in Malaga. Photo Alexander Liberman. *Harper's Bazaar*, October 15, 1964. © Alexander Liberman, © Hearst Corporation

37 "Goyasque" by Balenciaga. Kodachrome Richard Avedon. *Harper's Bazaar*, December 1949. © The Richard Avedon Foundation, © Hearst Corporation

38 Portrait of Mrs Harry Bull by Pavel Tchelitchew. *Harper's Bazaar*, March 1, 1941. © Pavel Tchelitchew, © Hearst Corporation

39 *Visionaire No. 37: Vreeland Memos*. New York: Visionaire Pub., 2001
Visionaire No. 37: Vreeland Memos, New York: Visionaire Pub., 2001
D.V. Edited by George Plimpton and Christopher Hemphill. New York: Alfred A. Knopf, 1984, pp. 49-50

40 Cloak, hat and muff in leopard by Molyneux. Photo George Hoyningen-Huene. *Harper's Bazaar*, September 15, 1939. © George Hoyningen-Huene, © Hearst Corporation

41 Toque in leopard by Schiaparelli. Photo George Hoyningen-Huene. *Harper's Bazaar*, September 15, 1939. © George Hoyningen-Huene, © Hearst Corporation

42 Page from the leading article "Vogue's eye view: Paris fashion report by Diana Vreeland" signed DV. Benedetta Barzini wears a leopard print and the model on the right a tiger print. Givenchy models. Photo Irving Penn. *Vogue*, September 15, 1969. © The Irving Penn Foundation, © Condé Nast

43 Page from the leading article "Paris: the news as we see it - a special Vogue report on the new French clothes" signed DV. Veruschka wears a giraffe printed nap coat by Guy Laroche. Photo Irving Penn. *Vogue*, September 1, 1965. © The Irving Penn Foundation, © Condé Nast

44 Coat by Yves Saint Laurent, 1969 autumn-winter collection. Photo by Duane Michals for *Yves Saint Laurent*, catalog for the exhibition curated by Diana Vreeland (New York, The Costume Institute at The Metropolitan Museum of Art, November 14, 1983-September 2, 1984). New York: The Metropolitan Museum of Art, 1983. © Duane Michals, © The Metropolitan Museum of Art

45 Diana Vreeland and her waitress Yvonne Duval Brown in the dining room of her Park Avenue apartment in New York. Photo Nicholas Vreeland. *Nest*, no. 7, winter 1999-2000. © Nicholas Vreeland, © Nest

46 "Black at the Baths of Tingo." Photo Toni Frissell. *Harper's Bazaar*, January 1952. © Toni Frissell, © Hearst Corporation

47 "All silk and yards wide". Photo Richard Avedon. *Harper's Bazaar*, June 1949. The picture is reprinted in the book by Diana Vreeland and Christopher Hemphill, *Allure*. New York: Doubleday, 1980. © The Richard Avedon Foundation, © Hearst Corporation

48 Cover photo, Kodachrome by Louise Dahl-Wolfe. Art direction Alexey Brodovitch. *Harper's Bazaar*, May 1948. © Louise Dahl-Wolfe, © Hearst Corporation

49 "Round-the-world Fashion: HB's Flying Odyssey." Photo Gleb Derujinsky. *Harper's Bazaar*, January 1958. © Gleb Durujinsky, © Hearst Corporation

50 Page from the leading article "Vogue's eye view of Paris... this is a love letter" signed DV. Marisa Berenson with feather hat by Lanvin. Photo Irving Penn. *Vogue*, September 15, 1967. © The Irving Penn Foundation, © Condé Nast

51 Cover: "to dazzle the Christmas eye, the jewel of the year - a huge, gilded pineapple helmet flaming with a ransom of diamonds... four-hundred-and-ninety-eight perfect blue-white stones in all. This cage of fantasy, designed especially for *Vogue* by Elizabeth Arden's young makeup wizard Pablo, and executed by Harry Winston." Photo Irving Penn. *Vogue*, December 1965. © The Irving Penn Foundation, © Condé Nast

52 Printed suit by Pucci. Photo Irving Penn. *Vogue*, October 15, 1965. © The Irving Penn Foundation, © Condé Nast

53 Hood in monkey fur by Revillon. Photo Irving Penn. *Vogue*, September 15, 1965. © The Irving Penn Foundation, © Condé Nast

54 Cover: "the ornamental zebra eye" by Pablo Manzoni of Elizabeth Arden. Photo Irving Penn. *Vogue*, September 15, 1964. © The Irving Penn Foundation, © Condé Nast

55 "A singular jewel", 1970. Photo David Bailey from the book *Allure*, produced by Diana Vreeland and Christopher Hemphill in 1980, and originally published in *Vogue*. © David Bailey, © Doubleday

56 *Allure*. With Christopher Hemphill. New York: Doubleday, 1980, p. 45
D.V. Edited by George Plimpton and Christopher Hemphill. New York: Alfred A. Knopf, 1984, p. 103
Memo of April 16, 1970. In *Visionaire No. 37: Vreeland Memos*. New York: Visionaire Pub., 2001
"Paris, the News as We See It," editorial from *Vogue*, September 1, 1965, p. 255

57 Isa Stoppi with make-up in arctic shades by Pablo Manzoni of Elizabeth Arden. Photo Gianni Penati. *Vogue*, September 15, 1967. © Gianni Penati, © Condé Nast

58 "Fashion is delicious." Photo Henry Rox. Art direction Alexey Brodovitch. *Harper's Bazaar*, June 1939. © Henry Rox, © Hearst Corporation

59 Portrait of Queen Marie Antoinette by Élisabeth Vigée Le Brun, 1778. Page from Olivier Bernier, *The Eighteenth-Century Woman* (New York: Doubleday - The Metropolitan Museum of Art, 1981), published on the occasion of the exhibition curated by Diana Vreeland (New York, The Costume Institute at The Metropolitan Museum of Art, December 16, 1981-September 5, 1982). © Doubleday, © The Metropolitan Museum of Art

60 Costume by Bob Mackie for Cher in *The Sonny and Cher Comedy Hour* (1973-1974). Photo by Keith Trumbo for the book by Dale McConathy and Diana Vreeland, *Hollywood Costume. Glamour! Glitter! Romance!* (New York: Harry N. Abrams, 1976), published after the exhibition *Romantic and Glamorous Hollywood Design* curated by Diana Vreeland (New York, The Costume Institute at The Metropolitan Museum of Art, November 21, 1974-August 31, 1975). © Keith Trumbo, © Harry N. Abrams

61 Costume by Travis Banton for Claudette Colbert in *Cleopatra* (directed by Cecil B. DeMille, 1934). Photo by Keith Trumbo for the book by Dale McConathy and Diana Vreeland, *Hollywood Costume. Glamour! Glitter! Romance!* (New York: Harry N. Abrams, 1976), published after the exhibition *Romantic and Glamorous Hollywood Design* curated by Diana Vreeland (New York, The Costume Institute at The Metropolitan Museum of Art, November 21, 1974-August 31, 1975). © Keith Trumbo, © Harry N. Abrams

62-63 Double page opening of the feature "Sheherazaderie: 12 pages of seraglio clothes to charm the sheik at home." Photo Irving Penn. *Vogue*, April 15, 1965. © The Irving Penn Foundation, © Condé Nast

64-65 "The eyes of the desert: Mme. Ahmed Benhima." Photo Richard Avedon. *Vogue*, September 15, 1969. © The Richard Avedon Foundation, © Condé Nast

66 Baroness Christa Humboldt with a *capote de paseo*, a cape worn by the *toreros* on their lap of honor around the arena. *Harper's Bazaar*, July 1941. © Hearst Corporation

67 Mel Ferrer as Luis Bello on the set of the film *The Brave Bulls* (directed by Robert Rossen, 1951). Photo Lippman. *Harper's Bazaar*, August 1950. © Lippman, © Hearst Corporation

68 "The art of pleasing." Photo Dennis Stock. *Harper's Bazaar*, April 1959. © Dennis Stock, © Hearst Corporation

69 Mirella Petteni wears a Ricci model with hairstyle by Kenneth. Photo Helmut Newton. *Vogue*, September 15, 1963. © Helmut Newton Foundation, © Condé Nast

70 Photo Louise Dahl-Wolfe. *Harper's Bazaar*, March 1957. © Louise Dahl-Wolfe, © Hearst Corporation

71 "When is a color an instant beautifier? When it's one that's as enhancing as a fresh make-up, bringing to the skin a look of creamy clarity." Photo Louise Dahl-Wolfe. The backgrounds with stylized ideograms were made by Dahl-Wolfe in her New York studio. *Harper's Bazaar*, April 1958. © Louise Dahl-Wolfe, © Hearst Corporation

72 "This is the blondeness as a goddess might wear it. This is how she must look sitting in a night club." Photo Richard Avedon. *Harper's Bazaar*, October 1957. © The Richard Avedon Foundation, © Hearst Corporation

73 Cover: a Kodachrome of Louise Dahl-Wolfe. Art direction Alexey Brodovitch. *Harper's Bazaar*, June 1944. © Louise Dahl-Wolfe, © Hearst Corporation

74 "Bravo, bravo, said her eyes to Penelope Tree when she opened them wide with color. What'll you have in the line of eye-opening entertaining?" Photo Richard Avedon. *Vogue*, August 15, 1969. © The Richard Avedon Foundation, © Condé Nast

75 Photo Louise Dahl-Wolfe. *Harper's Bazaar*, September 1956. © Louise Dahl-Wolfe, © Hearst Corporation

76-77 The jacquard knitwear by Missoni against the background of the Villa Chigi gardens at Castel Fusano. Photo Henry Clarke. *Vogue*, February 15, 1971. Rosita Missoni explains how in the autumn of 1968, Consuelo Crespi, Italian editor of *Vogue America*, organized her first meeting with Diana Vreeland in a suite at the Grand Hotel, Rome. Rosita arrived with her model to present the small collection of garments she had brought with her. But it was Consuelo Crespi herself who, when helping her take the clothes out of the suitcase, decided to act as model for the occasion. "Who better could have been asked for?" recalls Rosita Missoni. "A beautiful woman, of great elegance, a style that suited her perfectly and above all who loved our garments." On seeing those colored clothes when entering the suite from an adjoining room, Diana Vreeland picked one of them up and, pirouetting around the room, wrapped it around herself and exclaimed enthusiastically: "Who says there are seven colors? There are tones!" Following this positive meeting Diana Vreeland wrote a letter to Rosita and Ottavio Missoni, inviting them to New York the following spring. It was she who organized a meeting for them with the fashion coordinators of the leading department stores in New York, in which her editorial staff also participated in full. It was the collection's American debut, which the press renamed "Put Together." At the end of the presentation, emerging from the small and crowded suite and turning to the writers present, Diana Vreeland, pointing to Rosita and Tai, exclaimed: "These people are geniuses!"
This is the "quote" anecdote of Rosita Missoni's meeting with Diana Vreeland.
© Henry Clarke, © Condé Nast

78 Memo of 10 June 1970 on the subject of knitwear to the editorial staff at *Vogue*. Taken from *Visionaire n. 37: Vreeland Memos*. New York: Visionaire Pub., 2001. © Visionaire Pub.

79 Memo of 14 April 1969 on the subject of gray to the editorial staff at *Vogue*. Taken from *Visionaire n. 37: Vreeland Memos*. New York: Visionaire Pub., 2001. © Visionaire Pub.

80-81 Double page with garments by Mainbocher on the left and Vionnet on the right. Photo Man Ray. Art direction Alexey Brodovitch. *Harper's Bazaar*, September 15, 1937. © Man Ray Trust, © Hearst Corporation

82 Cover: a Kodachrome by Louise Dahl-Wolfe. Art direction Alexey Brodovitch. *Harper's Bazaar*, November 1949. © Louise Dahl-Wolfe, © Hearst Corporation

83 Cover: Wilhelmina Cooper with the anemone hat by Christian Dior. Photo Bert Stern. *Vogue*, February 1, 1964. © Bert Stern, © Condé Nast

84 "An Audrey Hepburn Fantasy" with the actress as Eliza Doolittle and the costumes designed by Cecil Beaton on the set of *My Fair Lady* (directed by George Cukor, 1964). Page conceived and created by Cecil Beaton. *Vogue*, December 1963. © Cecil Beaton, © Condé Nast

85 Costume by Cecil Beaton for Audrey Hepburn in *My Fair Lady* (directed by George Cukor, 1964). Photo by Keith Trumbo for the book by Dale McConathy and Diana Vreeland, *Hollywood Costume. Glamour! Glitter! Romance!* (New York:

Harry N. Abrams, 1976), published after the exhibition *Romantic and Glamorous Hollywood Design* curated by Diana Vreeland (New York, The Costume Institute at The Metropolitan Museum of Art, November 21, 1974-August 31, 1975). © Keith Trumbo, © Harry N. Abrams

86 Costume by Travis Banton for Mae West in *Belle of the Nineties* (directed by Leo McCarey, 1934). Photo by Keith Trumbo for the book by Dale McConathy and Diana Vreeland, *Hollywood Costume. Glamour! Glitter! Romance!* (New York: Harry N. Abrams, 1976), published after the exhibition *Romantic and Glamorous Hollywood Design* curated by Diana Vreeland (New York, The Costume Institute at The Metropolitan Museum of Art, November 21, 1974-August 31, 1975). © Keith Trumbo, © Harry N. Abrams

87 Madame X headdress for the Bal de Tête at the Ritz-Carlton. Photo Karen Radkai. *Harper's Bazaar*, November 1949. © Karen Radkai, © Hearst Corporation

88 Group of costumes by Irene Sharaff for the supporting actors in *The Pirate* (directed by Vincente Minnelli, 1948). Photo by Keith Trumbo for the book by Dale McConathy and Diana Vreeland, *Hollywood Costume. Glamour! Glitter! Romance!* (New York: Harry N. Abrams, 1976), published after the exhibition *Romantic and Glamorous Hollywood Design* curated by Diana Vreeland (New York, The Costume Institute at The Metropolitan Museum of Art, November 21, 1974-August 31, 1975). © Keith Trumbo, © Harry N. Abrams

89 Bird mask for the Bal Masqué at the Waldorf. Photo Karen Radkai. *Harper's Bazaar*, November 1949. © Karen Radkai, © Hearst Corporation

90 Costume by Edith Head for Hedy Lamarr in *Samson and Delilah* (directed by Cecil B. DeMille, 1949). Photo by Keith Trumbo for the book by Dale McConathy and Diana Vreeland, *Hollywood Costume. Glamour! Glitter! Romance!* (New York: Harry N. Abrams, 1976), published after the exhibition *Romantic and Glamorous Hollywood Design* curated by Diana Vreeland (New York, The Costume Institute at The Metropolitan Museum of Art, November 21, 1974-August 31, 1975). © Keith Trumbo, © Harry N. Abrams

91 Alla Nazimova in a scene from the film *Salomé* (directed by Charles Bryant, 1923) with the costume designed by Natacha Rambova. Taken from *Romantic and Glamorous Hollywood Design*, catalog of the exhibition curated by Diana Vreeland (New York, The Costume Institute at The Metropolitan Museum of Art, November 21, 1974-August 31, 1975). New York: The Metropolitan Museum of Art, 1974. © Keith Trumbo, © Harry N. Abrams

92-93 Double page dedicated to evening gowns by Alix (Madame Grès) on the left and Lelong on the right. Illustration by Lucha Truel. Art direction Alexey Brodovitch. *Harper's Bazaar*, September 15, 1937. © Lucha Truel, © Hearst Corporation

94 *Allure*. With Christopher Hemphill. New York: Doubleday, 1980, p. 11
Allure. With Christopher Hemphill. New York: Doubleday, 1980, p. 134
Allure. With Christopher Hemphill. New York: Doubleday, 1980, p. 134

95 Cocktail dress by Yves Saint Laurent, 1981 spring-summer collection. Photo by Duane Michals for *Yves Saint Laurent*, catalog of the exhibition curated by Diana Vreeland (New York, The Costume Institute at The Metropolitan Museum of Art, December 6, 1983-September 2, 1984). New York: The Metropolitan Museum of Art, 1983. © Duane Michals, © The Metropolitan Museum of Art, © Clarkson N. Potter

96-97 "The eye job", 1960s. Photo Elliott Erwitt/Magnum. Pages taken from the book *Allure* by Diana Vreeland and Christopher Hemphill (New York: Doubleday, 1980). © Elliott Erwitt/Magnum, © Doubleday

98 Photo John Chan. *Vogue*, September 1, 1967. © John Chan, © Condé Nast

99 Stage in the making of Dior mannequins at the Greneker Corporation. Photo Leslie Gill. Art direction Alexey Brodovitch. *Harper's Bazaar*, October 1948. © Leslie Gill, © Hearst Corporation

100 Evening gown by Alix (Madame Grès), circa 1938. Photo by Irving Penn for the photographic essay *Inventive Paris Clothes 1909-1939* (New York: The Viking Press, 1977) made with Diana Vreeland after the exhibition *The 10s, The 20s, The 30s: Inventive Clothes 1909-1939* curated by Diana Vreeland (New York, The Costume Institute at The Metropolitan Museum of Art, December 13, 1973-September 3, 1974). © The Irving Penn Foundation, © The Viking Press

101 "The body stocking - reward for diet restraint." Photo Helmut Newton. *Vogue*, October 15, 1964. © Helmut Newton Foundation, © Condé Nast

102-103 Double page dedicated to beauty. Photo Louise Dahl-Wolfe. Art direction Alexey Brodovitch. *Harper's Bazaar*, July 1941. © Louise Dahl-Wolfe, © Hearst Corporation

104-105 "Beauty Portraits." Photo Erwin Blumenfeld. Art direction Alexey Brodovitch. *Harper's Bazaar*, April 1942. © Erwin Blumenfeld, © Hearst Corporation

106 Photo Hiro Wakabayashi. *Harper's Bazaar*, April 1958. © Hiro Wakabayashi, © Hearst Corporation

107 Page "A golden glow the year round." Photo Ernst Beadle. Art direction Alexey Brodovitch. *Harper's Bazaar*, October 1946. © Ernst Beadle, © Hearst Corporation

108 Page dedicated to beauty with hairstyles by Hugh Harrison. Photo John Chan. *Vogue*, September 1, 1967. © John Chan, © Condé Nast

109 "The new spirit in appearance." Photo Leslie Gill. *Harper's Bazaar*, April 1946. © Leslie Gill, © Hearst Corporation

110 Greta Garbo, "the face that launched a thousand ships." Photo Antony Beauchamp. *Harper's Bazaar*, March 1958. © Antony Beauchamp, © Hearst Corporation

111 Gianni Agnelli photographed exclusively for *Vogue* at Villa Perosa by Ugo Mulas. *Vogue*, April 1, 1969. © Ugo Mulas, © Condé Nast

112 Page from the leading article "Vogue's first report on the new French clothes and the fresh excitement of Paris" signed DV. The model wears Yves Saint Laurent. Photo Irving Penn. *Vogue*, September 1, 1963. © The Irving Penn Foundation, © Condé Nast

113 Cher's hand. Photo Richard Avedon. *Vogue*, November 15, 1966. © The Richard Avedon Foundation, © Condé Nast

114 "Swimming by moonlight." Photo Louise Dahl-Wolfe. *Harper's Bazaar*, June 1939. © Louise Dahl-Wolfe, © Hearst Corporation

115 Statue of Florence Nightingale. *Harper's Bazaar*, March 1958. © Hearst Corporation

116 Kodachrome Martin Munkacsi. *Harper's Bazaar*, April 1950. © Martin Munkacsi, © Hearst Corporation

117 "The sphinx within": Marella Agnelli. Photo Richard Avedon. *Harper's Bazaar*, April 1960. © The Richard Avedon Foundation, © Hearst Corporation

118 Jacqueline Kennedy. Photo Larry Fried. *Vogue*, December 1965 © Larry Fried, © Condé Nast

119 "The outer eye [...] pretty exclamation points." Photo Gianni Penati. *Vogue*, April 1, 1969. © Gianni Penati, © Condé Nast

120 Two Vionnet models. Photo George Hoyningen-Huene. *Harper's Bazaar*, November 1936. © George Hoyningen-Huene, © Hearst Corporation

121 Veruschka in the feature "Journey to the light": "profile to the sun, right hair elongated with a young Egyptian god's sidelock" by Ara Gallant. Photo Franco Rubartelli. *Vogue*, April 1, 1967. © Franco Rubartelli, © Condé Nast

122 Photo Richard Avedon. *Harper's Bazaar*, February 1951. © The Richard Avedon Foundation, © Hearst Corporation

123 "Sizzling color, sea-cooled color." Photo Lillian Bassman. *Harper's Bazaar*, June 1954. © Lillian Bassman, © Hearst Corporation

124-125 "This thing called Pizzazz: an indefinable dynamic quality, the *je ne sais quoi* of function; as, for instance, adding Scotch put pizzazz into a drink. Certain clothes have it too." Art direction Alexey Brodovitch. *Harper's Bazaar*, March 1937. © Hearst Corporation

126 Nancy "Slim" Keith, at the time still Mrs Howard Hawks. Kodachrome John Engstead. *Harper's Bazaar*, August 1945. © John Engstead, © Hearst Corporation

127 "The neatest, slickest look around." Photo Genevieve Naylor. *Harper's Bazaar*, November 1950. © Genevieve Naylor, © Hearst Corporation

Style, catalog of the exhibition curated by Richard Martin and Harold Koda (New York, The Costume Institute at The Metropoltan Museum of Art, December 9, 1993-March 20, 1994). New York, The Metropolitan Museum of Art, 1993. © The Metropolitan Museum of Art

164   "The sphinx within": Gloria Vanderbilt in Mainbocher. Photo Richard Avedon. *Harper's Bazaar*, April 1960. © The Richard Avedon Foundation, © Hearst Corporation

165   Barbra Streisand: "Who else can decipher the myth of Streisand while it is still inside her?" Photo Bert Stern. *Vogue*, March 1. 1964. © Bert Stern, © Condé Nast

166   "Mrs Millicent Rogers emphasizes the chic." Kodachrome Louise Dahl-Wolfe. *Harper's Bazaar*, April 1948. © Louise Dahl-Wolfe, © Hearst Corporation

167   "Lauren Bacall in the infanta petticoat." Photo John Engstead. *Harper's Bazaar*, August 1945. © John Engsted, © Hearst Corporation

168   Rudolf Nureyev: "Surely this is genius." Photo Henry Cartier-Bresson. *Vogue*, March 1, 1964. © Henry Cartier-Bresson, © Condé Nast

169   Katharine Hepburn. Photo George Hoyningen-Huene. *Harper's Bazaar*, January 1940. © George Hoyningen-Huene, © Hearst Corporation

170   Marcello Mastroianni and Ursula Andress on the set of the film *The 10th Victim* (directed by Elio Petri, 1965). Photo Enzo Sellerio. *Vogue*, October 15, 1965. The photo was part of the feature "The man, the actor, the reluctant lover: Mastroianni", with an article by Luigi Barzini, exclusively for *Vogue*, which drew a profile of the actor. © Enzo Sellerio, © Condé Nast

171   Cover: "readying the great star, the great season. Sophia Loren, the Italian actress now appearing on *El Cid*, in a light, clear blue wool costume about to break into fall history." Behind her a young Halston adjusts her hat. Photo Richard Avedon. Art direction Henry Wolf. *Harper's Bazaar*, September 1961. © The Richard Avedon Foundation, © Hearst Corporation

172   Barbara "Babe" Paley: "She is an exception - who stands for exceptional things." Photo Richard Avedon. *Vogue*, May 1967. In her 1980 book *Allure*, Diana Vreeland says: "And when I talk about Babe Paley there is absolutely no snobbishness or sentimentalism. I talk about the line of her nose." © The Richard Avedon Foundation, © Condé Nast

173   "Here she is, Twiggy girl, on *Vogue*'s cover for the first time. She's one of the best summer looks around and she's wearing another [...] jersey beach cover by Grès." Photo Bert Stern. *Vogue*, April 15, 1967. © Bert Stern, © Condé Nast

174   "Beauty and the artist: the creation of a goddess. The great elegance and beauty of the Vicomtesse Jacqueline de Ribes inspire Raymundo de Larrain, director of the International Ballet of the Marquis de Cuevas, to create the delightfully fantastic maquillage and headdress". Evening gown by Grès. Photo Richard Avedon. *Harper's Bazaar*, September 1961. © The Richard Avedon Foundation, © Hearst Corporation

175   Queen Elizabeth II on the day of her coronation at Westminster, June 2, 1953. Photo British Information Office. *Harper's Bazaar*, June 1953. © British Information Office, © Hearst Corporation

176   Countess Mona Bismarck with a déshabillé by Balenciaga in her apartment at the Hotel Lombard, Paris. Photo Cecil Beaton. *Harper's Bazaar*, August 1955. © Cecil Beaton, © Hearst Corporation

177   Elizabeth Taylor in a flower caftan by Graziella Fontana, for the feature "Peter Glenville talks about the Burtons." Photo Henry Clarke. *Vogue*, September 1, 1967. © Henry Clarke, © Condé Nast

178   Maria Callas, 1958. Photo Anonymous/A.P. From the book *Allure*, by Diana Vreeland and Christopher Hemphill (New York: Doubleday, 1980). In the book Vreeland says: "If eyes were bullets, everyone in sight would be dead." The same picture of Callas was part of the moodboard in Vreeland's office at *Vogue*. © A.P., © Doubleday

179   *D.V.* Edited by George Plimpton and Christopher Hemphill. New York: Alfred A. Knopf, 1984, p. 27

182   Detail of an outfit by Yves Saint Laurent, spring-summer collection 1962. Photo by Duane Michals for *Yves Saint Laurent*, catalog of the exhibition curated by

Diana Vreeland (New York, The Costume Institute at The Metropolitan Museum of Art, December 6, 1983-September 2, 1984). New York: The Metropolitan Museum of Art, 1983. © Duane Michals, © The Metropolitan Museum of Art

183   Christopher Hemphill in his "Notes on a Collaboration," in *Allure*. New York: Doubleday, 1980, p. 9
Diana Vreeland in the "Notes on a Collaboration," in *Allure*. New York: Doubleday, 1980, p. 88

186   *Allure*. With Christopher Hemphill. New York: Doubleday, 1980, p. 24
Allure. With Christopher Hemphill. New York: Doubleday, 1980, p. 50

188   Preparation of the exhibition *The World of Balenciaga* curated by Diana Vreeland (New York, The Costume Institute at The Metropolitan Museum of Art, March 23, 1973-September 9, 1973). From Lisa Immordino Vreeland's book *Diana Vreeland: The Eye Has To Travel*. New York: Harry N. Abrams, 2011. © Lisa Immordino Vreeland

189   *D.V.* Edited by George Plimpton and Christopher Hemphill. New York: Alfred A. Knopf, 1984, p. 104

189   Matador's bolero, satin with gold embroidery, mid-19th century. Private collection of Martin Kamer, Switzerland

190   Correspondence between Diana Vreeland and Robert Mapplethorpe, September 1972. From *Diana Vreeland Papers 1899-2000*, The New York Public Library

190   from the top Detail of the mannequin with the costume designed by Irene Sharaff for Judy Garland in *The Pirate* (directed by Vincente Minnelli, 1948). Photo by Keith Trumbo for the book by Dale McConathy and Diana Vreeland, *Hollywood Costume. Glamour! Glitter! Romance!* (New York: Harry N. Abrams, 1976), published after the exhibition *Romantic and Glamorous Hollywood Design* curated by Diana Vreeland (New York, The Costume Institute at The Metropolitan Museum of Art, November 21, 1974-August 31, 1975). © Keith Trumbo, © Harry N. Abrams
Panorama of some mannequins in the exhibition *Romantic and Glamorous Hollywood Design* curated by Diana Vreeland (New York, The Costume Institute at The Metropolitan Museum of Art, November 21, 1974-August 31, 1975). © Keith Trumbo, © Harry N. Abrams
Detail of the mannequin with an outfit by Paquin, 1912. Photo by Irving Penn for the photographic essay *Inventive Paris Clothes 1909-1939* (New York: The Viking Press, 1977), published with Diana Vreeland after the exhibition *The 10s, The 20s, The 30s: Inventive Clothes 1909-1939* curated by Diana Vreeland (New York: The Costume Institute at The Metropolitan Museum of Art, December 13, 1973-September 3, 1974). © The Irving Penn Foundation, © The Viking Press
Cocktail dress by Yves Saint Laurent, fall-winter collection 1970-71. Photo by Duane Michals for *Yves Saint Laurent*, catalog of the exhibition curated by Diana Vreeland (New York, The Costume Institute at The Metropolitan Museum of Art, December 6, 1983-September 2, 1984). New York: The Metropolitan Museum of Art, 1983. © Duane Michals, © The Metropolitan Museum of Art

191   from the top Mannequin with dress by Poiret, 1910. Photo by Irving Penn for the photographic essay *Inventive Paris Clothes 1909-1939* (New York: The Viking Press, 1977), published with Diana Vreeland after the exhibition *The 10s, The 20s, The 30s: Inventive Clothes 1909-1939* curated by Diana Vreeland (New York, The Costume Institute at The Metropolitan Museum of Art, December 13, 1973-September 3, 1974). © The Irving Penn Foundation, © The Metropolitan Museum of Art
Detail of the mannequin with the costume designed by Orry-Kelly for Bette Davis in *The Private Lives of Elizabeth and Essex* (directed by Michael Curtiz, 1939). Photo by Keith Trumbo for the book by Dale McConathy and Diana Vreeland, *Hollywood Costume. Glamour! Glitter! Romance!* (New York: Harry N. Abrams, 1976), published after the exhibition *Romantic and Glamorous Hollywood Design* curated by Diana Vreeland (New York, The Costume Institute at The Metropolitan Museum of Art, November 21, 1974-August 31, 1975). © Keith Trumbo, © Harry N. Abrams

192   "Why Don't You...?" *Harper's Bazaar*, May 1941. © Hearst Corporation

192   *D.V.* Edited by George Plimpton and Christopher Hemphill. New York: Alfred A. Knopf, 1984, pp. 105-6

192   Preparation of the exhibition *The 10s, The 20s, The 30s: Inventive Clothes 1909-1939* curated by Diana Vreeland (New York, The Costume Institute at The Metropolitan Museum of Art, December 13, 1973-September 3, 1974). From Lisa

Immordino Vreeland's book *Diana Vreeland: The Eye Has To Travel*. New York: Harry N. Abrams, 2011. © Lisa Immordino Vreeland

193 from the top Double-page spread with two models by Alix (Madame Grès). Photo George Hoyningen-Huene. Art direction Alexey Brodovitch. *Harper's Bazaar*, August 1939. © George Hoyningen-Huene, © Hearst Corporation
Double-page spread "A New Perspective for Fall." Photo Ronny Jaques. Art direction Alexey Brodovitch. *Harper's Bazaar*, August 1946. © Ronny Jaques, © Hearst Corporation
Double-page spread with photo by Louise Dahl-Wolfe. Art direction Alexey Brodovitch. *Harper's Bazaar*, April 1947. © Louise Dahl-Wolfe, © Hearst Corporation

194 *D.V.* Edited by George Plimpton and Christopher Hemphill. New York: Alfred A. Knopf, 1984, p. 105

194 from the top Detail of dress from Yves Saint Laurent's "Russian" collection, fall-winter 1976-77. Photo by Duane Michals for *Yves Saint Laurent*, catalog of the exhibition curated by Diana Vreeland (New York, The Costume Institute at The Metropolitan Museum of Art, December 6, 1983-September 2, 1984). New York: The Metropolitan Museum of Art, 1983. © Duane Michals, © The Metropolitan Museum of Art
Traditional women's costumes for popular festivals, Central Russia, second half of 18th century. Photos courtesy of the State Hermitage Museum, Leningrad, and the State Historical Museum, Moscow. From *History of Russian Costume from the Eleventh to the Twentieth Century*, catalog of the exhibition *The Glory of Russian Costume* curated by Diana Vreeland (New York, The Costume Institute at The Metropolitan Museum of Art, December 9, 1976-September 6, 1977). New York: The Metropolitan Museum of Art, 1974. © The Metropolitan Museum of Art

196 Two mannequins with a peacock from the exhibition *The Manchu Dragon: Costumes of China—The Ch'ing Dynasty* curated by Diana Vreeland (New York, The Costume Institute at The Metropolitan Museum of Art, December 16, 1980-August 30, 1981). From Lisa Immordino Vreeland's book *Diana Vreeland: The Eye Has To Travel*. New York: Harry N. Abrams, 2011. © Lisa Immordino Vreeland

197 from the top Detail of the mannequin with the costume designed by Lady Duff-Gordon and then reproduced by Walter Plunkett for Ginger Rogers in *The Story of Vernon and Irene Castle* (directed by H.C. Potter, 1939). Photo by Keith Trumbo for the book by Dale McConathy and Diana Vreeland, *Hollywood Costume. Glamour! Glitter! Romance!* (New York: Harry N. Abrams, 1976), published after the exhibition *Romantic and Glamorous Hollywood Design* curated by Diana Vreeland (New York, The Costume Institute at The Metropolitan Museum of Art, November 21, 1974-August 31, 1975). © Keith Trumbo, © Harry N. Abrams
Mannequin with evening dress by Poiret, 1917. Photo by Irving Penn for the photographic essay *Inventive Paris Clothes 1909-1939* (New York: The Viking Press, 1977), published with Diana Vreeland following the exhibition *The 10s, The 20s, The 30s: Inventive Clothes 1909-1939* curated by Diana Vreeland (New York: The Costume Institute at The Metropolitan Museum of Art, December 13, 1973-September 3, 1974). © The Irving Penn Foundation, © The Viking Press

198 Preparation of the exhibition *Yves Saint Laurent* curated by Diana Vreeland (New York, The Costume Institute at The Metropolitan Museum of Art, December 6, 1983-September 2, 1984). From Lisa Immordino Vreeland's book *Diana Vreeland: The Eye Has To Travel*. New York: Harry N. Abrams, 2011. © Lisa Immordino Vreeland

199 Excerpt from a "Why Don't You...?" republished in John Esten, *Diana Vreeland Bazaar Years: Including 100 Audacious Why Don't Yous...?* New York: Universe Pub., 2001, p. 70

199 Sample of the Dalziel tartan made by Lochcarron of Scotland

203 Cover of *The World of Balenciaga*. Catalog of the exhibition curated by Diana Vreeland (New York, The Costume Institute at The Metropolitan Museum of Art, March 23-September 9, 1973). New York: The Metropolitan Museum of Art, 1973. © The Metropolitan Museum of Art

204 Cover of *The 10s, The 20s, The 30s: Inventive Clothes 1909-1939*. Catalog of the exhibition curated by Diana Vreeland (New York, The Costume Institute at The Metropolitan Museum of Art, December 13, 1973-September 3, 1974). New York: The Metropolitan Museum of Art, 1973. © The Metropolitan Museum of Art
Cover of Irving Penn and Diana Vreeland, *Inventive Paris Clothes 1909-1939*.

New York: The Viking Press, 1977. Published after the exhibition *The 10s, The 20s, The 30s: Inventive Clothes 1909-1939* curated by Diana Vreeland (New York, The Costume Institute at The Metropolitan Museum of Art, December 13, 1973-September 3, 1974). © The Viking Press
Cover of *Romantic and Glamorous Hollywood Design*. Catalog of the exhibition curated by Diana Vreeland (New York, The Costume Institute at The Metropolitan Museum of Art, November 21, 1974-August 31, 1975). New York: The Metropolitan Museum of Art, 1974. © The Metropolitan Museum of Art

205 Cover of Dale McConathy and Diana Vreeland, *Hollywood Costume. Glamour! Glitter! Romance!* New York: Harry N. Abrams, 1976. Published after the exhibition *Romantic and Glamorous Hollywood Design* curated by Diana Vreeland (New York, The Costume Institute at The Metropolitan Museum of Art, November 21, 1974-August 31, 1975). © Harry N. Abrams
Cover of *The American Women of Style: An Exhibition Organized by Diana Vreeland*. Catalog of the exhibition curated by Diana Vreeland (New York, The Costume Institute at The Metropolitan Museum of Art, December 18, 1975-August 31, 1976). New York: The Metropolitan Museum of Art, 1975. © The Metropolitan Museum of Art
Cover of *History of Russian Costume from the Eleventh to the Twentieth Century*. Catalog of the exhibition *The Glory of Russian Costume* curated by Diana Vreeland (New York, The Costume Institute at The Metropolitan Museum of Art, December 9, 1976-September 6, 1977). New York: The Metropolitan Museum of Art, 1974. © The Metropolitan Museum of Art

206 Cover of *Vanity Fair: Four Centuries of Fashion from the Costume Institute of the Metropolitan Museum of Art*. Catalog of the exhibition *Vanity Fair* curated by Diana Vreeland (St. Louis, St. Louis Art Museum, February 4- April 1, 1979). New York: The Metropolitan Museum of Art, 1979 (revised edition). © The Metropolitan Museum of Art
Cover of *Diaghilev: Costumes & Designs of the Ballets Russes*. Catalog of the exhibition curated by Diana Vreeland (New York, The Costume Institute at The Metropolitan Museum of Art, December 20, 1978-April 15, 1979). New York: The Metropolitan Museum of Art, 1978. © The Metropolitan Museum of Art
Cover of *The Imperial Style: Fashions of the Hapsburg Era*. Catalog of the exhibition *Fashions of the Hapsburg Era: Austria-Hungary* curated by Diana Vreeland (New York, The Costume Institute at The Metropolitan Museum of Art, December 11, 1979-August 31, 1980). New York: The Metropolitan Museum of Art, 1980. © The Metropolitan Museum of Art

207 Cover of *The Manchu Dragon: Costumes of the Ch'ing Dynasty, 1644-1912*. Catalog of the exhibition *The Manchu Dragon: Costumes of China—The Ch'ing Dynasty* curated by Diana Vreeland (New York, The Costume Institute at The Metropolitan Museum of Art, December 16, 1980-August 30, 1981). New York: The Metropolitan Museum of Art, 1980. © The Metropolitan Museum of Art
Cover of Olivier Bernier, *The Eighteenth-Century Woman*. Published on the occasion of the exhibition curated by Diana Vreeland (New York, The Costume Institute at The Metropolitan Museum of Art, December 16, 1981-September 5, 1982). New York: The Metropolitan Museum of Art-Doubleday, 1981. © Doubleday, © The Metropolitan Museum of Art

208 Cover of Philippe Jullian, *La Belle Époque: An Essay by Philippe Jullian, with Illustrations Selected by Diana Vreeland*. Catalog of the exhibition *La Belle Époque* curated by Diana Vreeland (New York, The Costume Institute at The Metropolitan Museum of Art, December 6, 1982-September 4, 1983). New York: The Metropolitan Museum of Art, 1982. © Doubleday, © The Metropolitan Museum of Art
Cover of *Yves Saint Laurent*. Catalog of the exhibition curated by Diana Vreeland (New York, The Costume Institute at The Metropolitan Museum of Art, December 6, 1983-September 2, 1984). New York: The Metropolitan Museum of Art - C.N. Potter, 1983. © The Metropolitan Museum of Art, © Clarkson N. Potter

209 Cover of Alexander Mackay-Smith, Jean R. Druesedow and Thomas Ryder, *Man and the Horse: An Illustrated History of Equestrian Apparel*. Catalog of the exhibition *Man and the Horse* curated by Diana Vreeland (New York, The Costume Institute at The Metropolitan Museum of Art, December 3, 1984-September 1, 1985). New York: The Metropolitan Museum of Art - Simon and Schuster, 1984. © The Metropolitan Museum of Art, Simon and Schuster
Cover of Louis Rousselet, *India of Rajahs*. With preface by Diana Vreeland. Milan: Franco Maria Ricci, 1985. Published in association with the exhibition *The Costumes of Royal India* curated by Diana Vreeland (New York: The Costume Institute at The Metropolitan Museum of Art, December 20, 1985-August 31, 1986). © Franco Maria Ricci

Cover of *The Costumes of Royal India Checklist*. Checklist of the exhibition curated by Diana Vreeland (New York: The Costume Institute at The Metropolitan Museum of Art, December 20, 1985-August 31, 1986). New York: Metropolitan Museum of Art, 1985. © The Metropolitan Museum of Art

Cover of Carol M. Wallace, Don McDonagh, Jean L. Druesedow, Laurence Libin and Constance Old, *Dance: A Very Social History*. With preface by Diana Vreeland. Catalog of the exhibition (New York, The Costume Institute at The Metropolitan Museum of Art, December 17, 1986-September 6, 1987). New York: The Metropolitan Museum of Art - Rizzoli, 1986. © The Metropolitan Museum of Art, Rizzoli

210 Homage to Diana Vreeland paid by Josh Gosfield on the occasion of the opening of the exhibition *Diana Vreeland: Immoderate Style* curated by Richard Martin and Harold Koda (New York, The Costume Institute at The Metropolitan Museum of Art, December 9, 1993-March 20, 1994). Page from *The New Yorker*, December 13, 1993. © Josh Gosfield, © Condé Nast

215 The first "Why Don't You...?" by Diana Vreeland. Art direction Alexey Brodovitch. *Harper's Bazaar*, March 1936. © Hearst Corporation

216-217 "Why Don't You...?" by Diana Vreeland on children. Art direction Alexey Brodovitch. *Harper's Bazaar*, August 1937. © Hearst Corporation

218-219 The last "Why Don't You...?" by Diana Vreeland on interior decorating. Art direction Alexey Brodovitch. *Harper's Bazaar*, May 1941. © Hearst Corporation

220-221 "Why Don't You...?" by Diana Vreeland on Christmas. Illustrations Erik Nitsche. Art direction Alexey Brodovitch. *Harper's Bazaar*, December 1936. © Erik Nitsche, © Hearst Corporation

222-223 Patricia Coffin, "Vogue's Diana Vreeland: She Sets the Fashion." Photos James H. Karales. *Look*, vol. 30, no. 1, January 11, 1966, pp. 56-7. © James H. Karales, © Cowles Media

224-225 Diana, Vreeland, "What is fashion?" *Look*, vol. 30, no. 1, January 11, 1966, p. 58. © Cowles Media

226-227 Ingeborg, Day, "Diana Vreeland: A Velvet Hand in an Iron Glove." *Ms.*, August 1975, pp. 24-5. © Liberty Media for Women, LLC

228 Joan, Kron, "Exhibition-ism: History as Fashion Power." *New York Magazine*, January 12, 1976, p. 78. © New York Media, LLC

238 *Santa Maria della Salute, Venice*. Watercolor by Raoul Dufy, 1938, from the estate of Diana Vreeland. Page from Sotheby's. *Property from the Estate of Diana D. Vreeland*. Auction catalog. New York: Sotheby's, 1990. © Sotheby's

238 *Allure*. With Christopher Hemphill. New York: Doubleday, 1980, p. 202. © Doubleday

Bibliography
EDITED BY VALENTINA MENEGHELLO

BOOKS AND ARTICLES
BY DIANA VREELAND

Vreeland, Diana, and Christopher Hemphill. *Allure*. New York: Doubleday, 1980

Vreeland, Diana. *D.V.*, ed. by George Plimpton and Christopher Hemphill. New York: Alfred A. Knopf, 1984

Vreeland, Diana. *D.V.: autobiografia*. Italian edition ed. by Antonio Siragusa e Domitilla Alessi. Palermo: Novecento, 2001

Vreeland, Diana. "What is fashion?" *Look*, vol. 30, no. 1, January 11, 1966, p. 58

Vreeland, Diana. *Diana Vreeland Papers 1899-2000*, The New York Public Library

EXHIBITION CATALOGS
AND PUBLICATIONS

The World of Balenciaga. Catalog of the exhibition curated by Diana Vreeland (New York, The Costume Institute at The Metropolitan Museum of Art, March 23-September 9, 1973). New York: The Metropolitan Museum of Art, 1973

The 10s, The 20s, The 30s: Inventive Clothes 1909-1939. Catalog of the exhibition curated by Diana Vreeland (New York, The Costume Institute at The Metropolitan Museum of Art, December 13, 1973- September 3, 1974). New York: The Metropolitan Museum of Art, 1973

Penn, Irving, with Diana Vreeland. *Inventive Paris Clothes 1909-1939*. New York: The Viking Press, 1977. Published after the exhibition *The 10s, The 20s, The 30s: Inventive Clothes 1909-1939* curated by Diana Vreeland (New York, The Costume Institute at The Metropolitan Museum of Art, December 13, 1973-September 3, 1974)

Romantic and Glamorous Hollywood Design. Catalog of the exhibition curated by Diana Vreeland (New York, The Costume Institute at The Metropolitan Museum of Art, November 21, 1974-August 31, 1975). New York: The Metropolitan Museum of Art, 1974

Romantic and Glamorous Hollywood Design Checklist. Checklist of the exhibition curated by Diana Vreeland (New York, The Costume Institute at The Metropolitan Museum of Art, November 21, 1974-August 31, 1975). New York: The Metropolitan Museum of Art, 1974

McConathy, Dale, with Diana Vreeland. *Hollywood Costume. Glamour! Glitter! Romance!* New York: Harry N. Abrams, 1976. Published following the exhibition *Romantic and Glamorous Hollywood Design* curated by Diana Vreeland (New York, The Costume Institute at the Metropolitan Museum of Art, November 21, 1974-August 31, 1975)

American Women of Style: An Exhibition Organized by Diana Vreeland. Catalog of the exhibition curated by Diana Vreeland (New York, The Costume Institute at The Metropolitan Museum of Art, December 18, 1975- August 31, 1976). New York: The Metropolitan Museum of Art, 1975

History of Russian Costume from the Eleventh to the Twentieth Century. Catalog of the exhibition *The Glory of Russian Costume* curated by Vreeland (New York, The Costume Institute at the Metropolitan Museum of Art, December 9,

1976-September 6, 1977). New York: The Metropolitan Museum of Art, 1974

Vanity Fair. Catalog of the exhibition *Vanity Fair: A Treasure Trove of the Costume Institute* curated by Diana Vreeland (New York, The Costume Institute at The Metropolitan Museum of Art, December 15, 1977-September 3, 1978). New York: The Metropolitan Museum of Art, 1977

Vanity Fair: Four Centuries of Fashion from the Costume Institute of the Metropolitan Museum of Art. Catalog of the exhibition *Vanity Fair* curated by Diana Vreeland (St. Louis, St. Louis Art Museum, February 4-April 1, 1979). New York: The Metropolitan Museum of Art, 1979 (revised edition)

Diaghilev: Costumes & Designs of the Ballets Russes. Catalog of the exhibition curated by Diana Vreeland (New York, The Costume Institute at The Metropolitan Museum of Art, December 20, 1978-April 15, 1979). New York: The Metropolitan Museum of Art, 1978

The Imperial Style: Fashions of the Hapsburg Era. Catalog of the exhibition *Fashions of the Hapsburg Era: Austria-Hungary* curated by Diana Vreeland (New York, The Costume Institute at The Metropolitan Museum of Art, December 1979-August 1980). New York: The Metropolitan Museum of Art, 1980

The Manchu Dragon: Costumes of the Ch'ing Dynasty, 1644-1912. Catalog of the exhibition *The Manchu Dragon: Costumes of China—The Ch'ing Dynasty* curated by Diana Vreeland (New York, The Costume Institute at The Metropolitan Museum of Art, December 16, 1980-August 30, 1981). New York: The Metropolitan Museum of Art, 1980

Ettesvold, Paul M. *The Eighteenth-Century Woman: An Exhibition at the Costume Institute*. Catalog and checklist of the exhibition curated by Diana Vreeland (New York, The Costume Institute at The Metropolitan Museum of Art, December 16, 1981-September 5, 1982). New York: The Metropolitan Museum of Art, 1981

Bernier, Olivier. *The Eighteenth-Century Woman*. Published on the occasion of the exhibition curated by Diana Vreeland (New York, The Costume Institute at The Metropolitan Museum of Art, December 16, 1981-September 5, 1982). New York: Doubleday & Company - The Metropolitan Museum of Art, 1981

Jullian, Philippe. *La Belle Époque: An Essay by Philippe Jullian*. With illustrations selected by Diana Vreeland. Catalog of the exhibition *La Belle Époque* curated by Diana Vreeland (New York, The Costume Institute at The Metropolitan Museum of Art, December 6, 1982-September, 4 1983). New York: The Metropolitan Museum of Art, 1982

Ettesvold, Paul M. *La Belle Époque, Exhibition Checklist: A Checklist to the Exhibition at the Costume Institute, December 6, 1982 through September 4, 1983*. With an introduction by Stella Blum. Checklist of the exhibition *La Belle Époque* curated by Diana Vreeland (New York, The Costume Institute at The Metropolitan Museum of Art, December 6, 1982-September 4, 1983). New York: The Metropolitan Museum of Art, 1983

Yves Saint Laurent. Catalog of the exhibition curated by Diana Vreeland (New York, The Costume Institute at The Metropolitan Museum of Art, December 6, 1983-September 2, 1984). New York: The Metropolitan Museum of Art - C.N. Potter, 1983

Mackay-Smith, Alexander, Jean R. Druesedow and Thomas Ryder. *Man and the Horse: An Illustrated History of Equestrian Apparel*. Catalog of the exhibition *Man and the Horse* curated by Diana Vreeland (New York, The Costume Institute at The Metropolitan Museum of Art, December 18, 1984-September 1, 1985). New York: The Metropolitan Museum of Art - Simon and Schuster, 1984

Rousselet, Louis. *India of Rajahs*. With a preface by Diana Vreeland. Milan: Franco Maria Ricci, 1985. Published in association with the exhibition *The Costumes of Royal India* curated by Diana Vreeland (New York, The Costume Institute at The Metropolitan Museum of Art, December 20, 1985-August 31, 1986)

The Costumes of Royal India Checklist. Checklist of the exhibition curated by Diana Vreeland (New York, The Costume Institute at The Metropolitan Museum of Art, December 20, 1985-August 31, 1986). New York: The Metropolitan Museum of Art, 1985

Wallace, Carol McD., Don McDonagh, Jean L. Druesedow, Laurence Libin and Constance Old. *Dance a Very Social History*. With a preface by Diana Vreeland. Catalog of the exhibition (New York, The Costume Institute at The Metropolitan Museum of Art, December 17, 1986-September 6, 1987). New York: The Metropolitan Museum of Art - Rizzoli, 1986

BOOKS WITH A CONTRIBUTION FROM DIANA VREELAND

Vogue Poster Book. With an introduction by Diana Vreeland. New York: Harmony Press, 1975

Berenson, Marisa. *Dressing Up: How to Look and Feel Absolutely Perfect for Any Social Occasion*. With an introduction by Diana Vreeland. New York: Putnam, 1984

Carter, Ernestine. *The Changing World of Fashion: 1900 to the Present*. With an introduction by Diana Vreeland. London: Weidenfeld and Nicolson, 1977

Damase, Jacques. *Sonia Delaunay, Her Art and Fashion*. With an introduction by Diana Vreeland. New York: G. Braziller, 1985

Horst. *Vogue's Book of Houses, Gardens, People*. Texts by Valentine Lawford and an introduction by Diana Vreeland. London: Bodley Head, 1968

Manzoni, Pablo. *Instant Beauty: The Complete Way to Perfect Makeup*. With an introduction by Diana Vreeland. New York: Simon and Schuster, 1978

Smith, Jane S. *Elsie de Wolfe: A Life in the High Style*. With a preface by Diana Vreeland. New York: Atheneum, 1982

Yamanobe, Tomoyuki (ed.). *Opulence: The Kimonos and Robes of Itchiku Kubota*. With a message from Diana Vreeland. Tokyo: Kodansha International, 1984

BOOKS ON DIANA VREELAND

Louise Dahl-Wolfe. New York: Harry N. Abrams, 2000

Visionaire No. 37: Vreeland Memos, New York: Visionaire Pub., 2001

Beaton, Cecil. *The Glass of Fashion*. New York: Doubleday & Company, 1954

Dwight, Eleanor. *Diana Vreeland*. New York: HarperCollins, 2002

Esten, John. *Diana Vreeland Bazaar Years: Including 100 Audacious Why Don't Yous…?* New York: Universe Pub., 2001

Hampton, Mark, and Mary Louise Wilson. *Full Gallop*. New York: Dramatists Play Service, 1997

Immordino Vreeland, Lisa. *Diana Vreeland: The Eye Has To Travel*. New York: Harry N. Abrams, 2011

Martin, Richard, and Harold Koda (eds.). *Diana Vreeland: Immoderate Style*. Catalog of the exhibition curated by Richard Martin and Harold Koda (New York, The Costume Institute at The Metropolitan Museum of Art, December 9, 1993-March 20, 1994). New York: The Metropolitan Museum of Art, 1993

Rense, Paige (ed.). *Celebrity Homes: Architectural Digest Presents the Private Worlds of Thirty International Personalities*. New York: The Viking Press, 1977

Rogers, Peter. *What Becomes a Legend Most: The Blackglama Story*. With photos by Richard Avedon and Bill King. New York: Simon and Schuster, 1979

Silverman, Debora. *Selling Culture: Bloomingdale's, Diana Vreeland, and the New Aristocracy of Taste in Reagan's America*. New York: Pantheon Books, 1986

Sotheby's. *Property from the Estate of Diana D. Vreeland*. Auction catalog. New York: Sotheby's, 1990

Sotheby's. *The Diana Vreeland Collection of Fashion Jewelry*. Auction catalog. New York: Sotheby's, 1987

Tapert, Annette, and Diana Edkins. *The Power of Style: The Women Who Defined the Art of Living Well*. New York: Crown, 1994

Warburg Roosevelt, Felicia. *Doers & Dowagers*. New York: Doubleday & Company, 1975

Warhol, Andy. *Andy Warhol's Exposures*. Photos by Andy Warhol; text by Andy Warhol with Bob Colacello. New York: Grosset & Dunlap, 1979

Weber, Bruce. *A House Is Not a Home*. Boston: Bulfinch Press, 1996

ARTICLES ON DIANA VREELAND

"Diana Vreeland Knows How to Pack a Museum." *People*, December 9, 1974, p. 14

"Diana Vreeland, 550 Park Avenue, New York." *Nest*, no. 7, winter 1999-2000, pp. 54-67

"Diana Vreeland: Fashion's Empress Decrees a Delicious Occasion." *New York Magazine*, December 17, 1977, p. 95

Alhadeff, Gini. "Geniale e unica. Mrs. Diana Vreeland." *Vogue Italia*, special issue no. 23, September 1988

Cocks, Jay. "Living: Puttin' on the Ritz in Gotham." *Time*, January 10, 1983

Cocks, Jay, and Elizabeth Rudulph. "Living: A Harmony of Fugitive Color." *Time*, December 16, 1985

Coffin, Patricia. "Vogue's Diana Vreeland: She Sets the Fashion." With photos by James H. Karales. *Look*, vol. 30, no. 1, January 11, 1966, pp. 56-7

Day, Ingeborg. "Diana Vreeland: A Velvet Hand in an Iron Glove." *Ms.*, August 1975, pp. 24-30

Drier, Melissa. "Haute Exposition. Interview with Harold Koda." *Acne Paper*, no. 3, autumn 2006, pp. 108-14

Duffy, Martha. "Living: Toasting Saint Laurent." *Time*, December 12, 1983

Goodman, Wendy. "Man & the Horse: Diana Vreeland's Latest Costume Extravaganza." *New York Magazine*, November 26, 1984, pp. 65-72

Kornbluth, Jesse. "The Empress of Clothes." *New York Magazine*, November 29, 1982, pp. 30-6

Kron, Joan. "Exhibition-ism: History as Fashion Power." *New York Magazine*, January 12, 1976, p. 78

Lieberson, Jonathan. "Empress of Fashion: Diana Vreeland." *Interview*, no. 12, December 1980

Morris, Bernardine. "Gala Night at Met Hails Saint Laurent." *The New York Times*, December 6, 1983

Palmer, Alexandra. "Untouchable. Creating Desire and Knowledge in Museum Costume and Textile Exhibitions." *Fashion Theory: The Journal of Dress, Body & Culture*, vol. 12, no. 1, 2008, pp. 31-63

Perelman, S.J. "Frou-Frou, or the Future of Vertigo." *The New Yorker*, April 16, 1938, p. 17

Plimpton, George. "Diana Vreeland." *Interview*, vol. XIV, no. 12, December 1984, pp. 81-3

Steele, Valerie. "Museum Quality. The Rise of the Fashion Exhibition." *Fashion Theory: The Journal of Dress, Body & Culture*, vol. 12, no. 1, 2008, pp. 7-30

Stevenson, N.J. "The Fashion Retrospective." *Fashion Theory: The Journal of Dress, Body & Culture*, vol. 12, no. 2, 2008, pp. 219-36

Storr, Robert. "Unmaking History at the Costume Institute." *Art in America*, no. 75, February 1987, pp. 15-23

Talley, André Leon. "Vreeland's Show." *The New York Times*, December 6, 1981, p. 192

Tolini Finamore, Michelle. "Diana Vreeland." In *Encyclopedia of Clothing and Fashion*, ed. by Valerie Steele. Detroit: Charles Scribner's Sons, 2005, vol. 3, pp. 406-8

Trow, George W.S., and Natacha Stewart. "The Talk of the Town: Notes and Comment." *The New Yorker*, December 2, 1976, pp. 27-30

Trow, George W.S. "Haute, Haute, Couture." *The New Yorker*, May 26, 1975, pp. 81-8

Trow, George W.S. "The Talk of the Town: Inventive." *The New Yorker*, December 24, 1973, pp. 31-2

Trow, George W.S. "The Talk of the Town: Turnout." *The New Yorker*, December 17, 1979, p. 38

Trow, George W.S. "The Talk of the Town: Women of Style." *The New Yorker*, December 29, 1975, pp. 15-6

Weymouth, Lally. "A Question of Style. A Conversation with Diana Vreeland." *Look*, vol. 30, no. 1, January 11, 1966, pp. 38-53

Wintour, Anna. "La Belle Époque." With illustrations by Alexander S. Vethers. *New York Magazine*, November 29, 1982, pp. 38-41

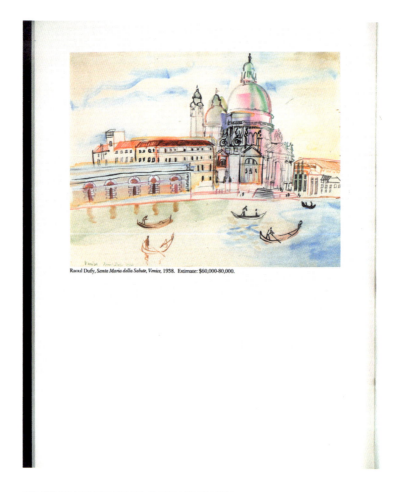

Raoul Dufy, *Santa Maria della Salute, Venice*, 1938. Estimate: $60,000-80,000.

"WHAT DO YOU THINK OF JEANS," THEY SAY.

OF COURSE THEY EXPECT ME TO RELEASE MYSELF AND SAY,
"OH, THEY'RE TERRIBLE! THEY'VE KILLED FASHION!"
WHEREAS, ACTUALLY, BLUE JEANS ARE THE ONLY THINGS THAT HAVE KEPT
FASHION ALIVE BECAUSE THEY'RE MADE OF A MARVELOUS FABRIC AND THEY
HAVE FIT AND DASH AND LINE...
THE ONLY IMPORTANT INGREDIENT OF FASHION.

SO, I ALWAYS SAY THE SAME THING. I SAY, "THEY'RE THE MOST BEAUTIFUL
THINGS SINCE THE GONDOLA," AND LEAVE IT AT THAT.

Diana Vreeland